SHAKESPEARE AND THE AWARENESS OF THE AUDIENCE

SHAKESPEARE AND THE AWARENESS OF THE AUDIENCE

Ralph Berry

St. Martin's Press   New York

All rights reserved. For information, write:
St. Martin's Press, Inc., 175 Fifth Avenue, New York, NY 10010
Printed in Hong Kong
Published in the United Kingdom by The Macmillan Press Ltd.
First published in the United States of America in 1985

ISBN 0-312-71423-8

Library of Congress Cataloging in Publication Data

Berry, Ralph, 1931–
    Shakespeare and the awareness of the audience.

    Includes bibliographical references and index.
    1. Shakespeare, William, 1564–1616 – Criticism and
interpretation – Addresses, essays, lectures.   2. Shakespeare,
William, 1564–1616 – Stage history – To 1625 – Addresses,
essays, lectures.   3. Theater – Great Britain – History –
Addresses, essays, lectures.   4. Theater audiences – Addresses,
essays, lectures.   5. Masques – Addresses, essays, lectures.
I. Title.
PR2976.B423   1985   822.3′3   84-9772
ISBN 0-312-71423-8

For Mary

Contents

Acknowledgements

Chapter 1, "Metamorphoses of the Stage", first appeared in *Shakespeare Quarterly*. Chapter 2, "Richard III: Bonding the Audience", was published in *The Mirror up to Shakespeare: Essays in Honour of G. R. Hibbard,* ed. J. C. Gray (University of Toronto Press). The chapters on *The Merchant of Venice, Twelfth Night* and *Julius Caesar* (Chapters 4–6) appeared in *Thalia, Shakespeare Survey* and *Dalhousie Review,* respectively; that on "Masques and Dumb Shows in Webster" in *Elizabethan Theatre,* vol. VII, ed. G. R. Hibbard, published by P. D. Meany in Canada and The Shoe String Press in the USA. I am grateful to the Editors and Presses for their permission to reprint this material.

R.B.

Introduction

The awareness of an audience settled in a theatre is not that of a reader over his book. It is substantially a group awareness; there is a merging of consciousnesses; doors are thrown open which even the practised reader can never hope to do more than push slightly ajar. The human mind has been likened in a great simile to the city of Rome – as that city would be if every stage of its development were preserved in strata, the Rome of each succeeding age superincumbent upon the Rome of the last. It seems to be of some such greater and continuing city that we are made free in the theatre, and much is comprehensible there that must begin to perplex us when we emerge. Does this wider citizenship, this driving of shafts, as it were, deep into the mind, constitute the cathartic function of drama; and is the growth of such a science as Freud's, therefore, a function of the atrophy of such great public arts as Shakespeare's?

J. I. M. Stewart[1]

The "awareness of an audience" is the magnetic pole of this book. Such a topic defies close description, or precise navigational aids. The audience is always shifting, always amorphous. The theatre of Shakespeare's day embraced a range of playhouse, playwright, acting corps, audiences: *Shakespeare's Audience* (the title is Harbage's) is for practical purposes a fair generalization, but begs many questions. What was the overlap with Dekker's audience? How large was the proportion of constant Shakespeare supporters? Were playhouse loyalties ingrained, and did the Red Bull people often attend the Globe? Even on the most literal of demographic bases, we cannot be sure of the London audience's composition. The latest argument (Ann Jennalie Cook's *The Privileged Playgoers of Shakespeare's London 1576–1642*)[2] holds that Shakespeare's audience was not the wide social sampling of myth, but a largely middle and upper class grouping. By *Henry VIII* (1613), that class audience was overtly acknowledged in the text of the play. But the demographic or local nature of the audience is not a main concern of this book. The audience is an eternal puzzle, even when we are part of it. What the audience is, no man knows. It has assembled for a single occasion and will never meet again. Even so, the playwright knows or guesses something of it. He must have a strategy for bringing this curious multiple into a union of sorts. He must, like an actor – and Shakespeare was an actor – play to all parts of the house, so as to induce in them their share of the common experience.

That experience is what I pursue in the studies that make up this book. Shakespeare's plays are the most successful programmes for uniting audiences that we have record of. They must, I think, proceed from the assumption that there is a single collective mind for the playwright to influence, however disparate the individuals who compose that mind. But there is no single master secret of strategy. Northrop Frye sees the plays "like a number of simul-taneous chess games played by a master who wins them all by devices familiar to him, and gradually, with patient study, to us, but which remain mysteries of an unfathomable skill".[3] I have no ambition to achieve a larger synthesis of such devices. It is sufficient, for me, to describe a single programme by which Shakespeare works on the minds of his audience.

Hence this book offers a series of explorations, not a sustained argument. In the first essay, I describe some implications of the stage's physical impact, a platform thrusting in upon the audience like a ship, a promontory, an island, even a cliff. That platform, and the audience consciousness of it, must have energized far more passages in the text than we can imagine. The essays that follow explore the social, or tribal consciousness of the audience in certain plays. *Richard III* draws upon the scattered origins of the audience, and uses topography to create a national unity. *The Comedy of Errors* is a palimpsest of experience, with Roman silting onto Greek as the cultural metaphor for that experience. It is England, with its subliminal assurances of home, that helps to stabilize the chaotic suggestions of *The Comedy of Errors*. In *The Merchant of Venice*, the thrust of the subliminal suggestions is to disturb the audience, and I analyse the play in terms of simple discomfort. Disturbance and assurance is a major spectrum within which Shakespeare organizes his effects. *Twelfth Night* is based on a denial of expectations: the play proposes a conventional plot and sub-plot, romantic and comic, then mutates to the point of assertion that the comic action is the major one. *Twelfth Night* reaches the visceral excitements of blood sport, as the audience realizes that it is the *pack* engaged in baiting Malvolio – this in a theatre (Globe) which may well have staged bear-baitings, as other theatres certainly did. Communal identity does not have to be a cheery, reassuring affair, and *Julius Caesar* supplies a particularly bleak model. It is a tragedy of communal violence, whose rituals stem from a rigid enforcement of Roman identity.

The last three essays circle round the masque, the salient dramatic form of the Jacobean theatre. Webster was fascinated with the ironic and subversive possibilities of the masque; for him, masque and dumb show were emblems of the glittering corruption of State. Such a perception was not unique to Webster, but current in the second decade of the seventeenth century. With Shakespeare, the masque called forth a more balanced and wide-ranging appraisal, and he exploits its possibilities in the final romances without limiting himself to an *idée fixe*. *Henry VIII* is perfectly aware of the masque as a device of State – and of the need to let the people in. The masque is still a great show, the qualities of which the play celebrates at numerous points. Shakespeare's sense of the masque relates easily to his general response to chivalry, an oscillation between the extremes of irony and elegy. The middle range is an awareness of chivalry that includes admiration for its glamour, and a cool analysis of its inner contradictions. Chivalry, for all its stage glitter, is by *Troilus and Cressida* the surface of a defunct ideology, yet another form of illusion destined to perish. All the same, *Troilus and Cressida* avoids an outright dismissal of chivalry, and the eternal ambivalence of Shakespeare leaves some options open at the end. For the audience, the play is both archaism and topicality, and thus an image of the world it knows. Chivalry and masque are at once the real world, the world of Essex and Inigo Jones, and the costume drama of the mind.

1 Metamorphoses of the Stage

Nay, when you look into my galleries,
How bravely they're trimmed up, you all shall swear
You're highly pleas'd to see what's set down there:
Stories of men and women, mix'd together,
Fair ones with foul, like sunshine in wet weather;
Within one square a thousand heads are laid,
So close that all of heads the room seems made;
As many faces there, fill'd with blithe looks,
Shew like the promising titles of new books
Writ merrily, the readers being their own eyes,
Which seem to move and to give plaudities;
And here and there, whilst with obsequious ears
Throng'd heaps do listen, a cut-purse thrusts and leers
With hawk's eyes for his prey, I need not shew him;
By a hanging, villainous look yourselves may know him,
The face is drawn so rarely: then, sir, below,
The very floor, as 'twere, waves to and fro,
And, like a floating island, seems to move
Upon a sea bound in with shores above.

All   These sights are excellent!

Dekker and Middleton, *The Roaring Girl* (c. 1608)

The Elizabethan stage can be anything in this world or the next: a battlefield, the Court, the underworld. The self-enclosed, self-sufficient world of the play is a primary convention. Against that lies a set of conventions much explored in recent years, particularly since Anne Righter's *Shakespeare and the Idea of the Play* (London: Chatto & Windus, 1962). Such conventions challenge or subvert the autonomy of the play world. They include choric speeches, together with prologue and epilogue. They permit direct address to

1

the audience by clowns (Launce with his dog) and lineal descendants of the Vice (Richard III, Iago). Sometimes the stage draws attention to itself explicitly – "this unworthy scaffold", "this wooden O" – or through the subtler provocations of "this great stage of fools" and "the great globe itself". The reflexive staginess of the Elizabethan drama is a well-understood phenomenon now, and we have learned to be alert to "act", "scene", "play", "perform", and so on, as they occur in the text of a play. Through them we understand a fundamental premise of Elizabethan dramaturgy, that the stage is also a stage.

I want here to discuss some transformations of the stage that are neither plainly reflexive nor totally submissive to the autonomy of the play world. I have in mind a series of images in the play-text that are activated by the physical facts of the stage, and thus create a composite image of word and setting. The audience is linked to the action through the nature of the playhouse itself. The "Elizabethan Playhouse", as we know, did not exist: there is no stereotype model. For my purposes here, however, it is enough to extract the (apparent) salient feature of De Witt's sketch of the Swan: a raised platform, which would be lapped on three sides by the audience, some standing and some seated in the galleries. That is all I need to pursue the fundamental metaphors of relationship.

I

What did the audience look like? Dekker – or Middleton – tells us in the extraordinarily suggestive metaphor I have quoted at the beginning.[1] The heads of the standing spectators, moving to and fro for a better view (like the soldiers in *Alexander Nevsky*),[2] seemed to him a "floating island", which moved "upon a sea bound in with shores above". The viewpoint is unidentified, but it is surely that from the stage. We have an actor's perception of audience. It is not, I think, a metaphor capable of development, for the position of the actors has no base in the metaphor: are they at sea, on a boat, on land? The audience, for its part, would not *feel* like a "floating island". It might passingly relish the conceit, as spoken by Sir Alexander Wengrave.[3] But there are no subterranean bonds between actors and audience to be tightened this way. The "floating island" image, vivid though it is, has nowhere to go.

Reverse the direction of the communication, and everything changes. What matters is the stage, and how it appears to the audience. The concrete reality of the platform, as perceived by the spectators, must energize certain passages in the text. Let us begin with Dekker's *The Whore of Babylon* (1606), whose concluding lines are

> *Titania*   Thankes *Time* for this; lanch forth to *Oberons* vayle.
> We are neere shore: your hands to strike our saile.
>
> *Exeunt.*
>
> (v. vi. 138–9)[4]

The last scene is set in Titania's camp (Tilbury). Through the offices of Time, the audience is permitted to take in the reactions of the Empress to her naval defeat (the Armada). Her exit line intimates a nautical setting, one which is in keeping with the tenor of *The Whore of Babylon*, for two previous scenes (v. iv and v. v) have been set at sea for the sea fight. So the traditional appeal for applause is nicely pointed here. The platform stage is a *ship*, nearing shore, and the audience is elliptically called upon to leave the shore, clamber aboard, and help strike sail. The dynamics of the transaction draw forth applause as the response; it is impossible to guess whether Dekker expected, or conventions permitted, the more excitable of the audience to mount upon the stage. They may have reached up to grasp the hands of the actors. The correspondence of platform and ship's deck is active here, in the formal climax of actor–audience relationship.

A similar correspondence occurs at the end of *Westward Ho!* (1604). The final song, "Oares, Oares, Oares, Oares", suggests, surely through mime as well as words, the stage–boat metaphor. It runs:

> Oares, Oares, Oares, Oares,
> To London hay, to London hay:
> Hoist up sayles and lets away,
> For the safest bay
> For us to land is London shores.
> Oares, Oares, Oares, Oares:
> Quickly shall wee get to Land,
> If you, if you, if you,
> Lend us but halfe a hand,
> O lend us halfe a hand.
>
> *Exeunt.*
>
> (v. iv. 309–18)[5]

Are the actors reaching out for the hands of the spectators, as
though the great *boat* of the stage were driving in upon the shore?
The strong, metronomic pulses of "Oares, Oares, Oares, Oares",
culminating in the kinetic urgency of "if you, if you, if you", implies,
I think, a response beyond mere applause. The verbal splicing of
"hand" brings together disparate activities, and I suppose that the
audience is to clap its hands and reach out towards the actors. We
are left, as in *The Whore of Babylon*, with the basic element of the
situation: the self-contained bulk of the platform approximates to
the deck of a boat or ship. It is a correspondence necessarily
undeveloped, and is used here for a special effect only.

II

The natural container for such a correspondence is the ship scene,
which places the action formally aboard ship. I do not find among
the authorities a sustained treatment of ship scenes in Elizabethan
and Stuart drama. Sir Edmund Chambers touches the subject
passingly,[6] and lists four plays only: *Antony and Cleopatra*, *Pericles*, *The
Tempest* and *The First part of the Contention betwixt the two famous Houses
of Yorke and Lancaster*. It is perhaps misleading to cite scene xii of *1
Contention* as a "ship" scene. It is true that the stage direction reads
(in the 1594 edition) *Alarmes within, and the chambers be discharged, like
as it were a fight at sea. And then enter the Captaine of the ship and the
Maister and the Maisters Mate, & the Duke of Suffolke disguised*. The
scene opens with the Captain's "Bring forward these prisoners that
scornd to yeeld, / Unlade their goods with speed, and sinke their
ship", and thus permits the assumption that Suffolk's arraignment
occurs on ship. But the corresponding scene in *2 Henry VI* (IV. i)
makes it plain that the action occurs on shore. The stage direction is
similar: *Alarum. Fight at sea. Ordnance goes off*. The Lieutenant's
orders, however, identify the location decisively:

> Therefore bring forth the soldiers of our prize;
> For, whilst our pinnace anchors in the Downs,
> Here shall they make their ransom on the sand,
> Or with their blood stain this discolored shore.
>
> (IV. i. 8–11)

Shakespeare's three plays with ship scenes are all Jacobean; and the development of ship scenes seems to have been a feature of Stuart drama, though they are not exclusive to that era. Richard Southern quotes from the anonymous *Pleasant Comedie called Common Conditions* (1576): "on two occasions characters have to board vessels, or escape from being tossed overboard into raging seas. But in this play the effect of the ship is conveyed by shouts off."[7] Taking *Common Conditions* with the murky staging of *1 Contention*, one can assert the existence of some kind of Elizabethan tradition of ship scenes, even if that tradition was neither strong nor developed.

The Stuart development of the ship-scene tradition was technically resourceful, but it extends beyond the limits of my subject here. Since I concentrate on analogues to the platform itself, I do not wish to pursue the issue of ship scenes that develop further correspondences. John Cranford Adams enumerates "a series of ship scenes in which the platform stage serves as the main deck, the tarras [projecting balcony] as the raised quarter deck, and the music gallery as the main-top or crow's nest".[8] The main instances he cites, Heywood and Rowley's *Fortune by Land and Sea* (Red Bull, 1607–9) and Fletcher and Massinger's *The Double Marriage* (Globe and Blackfriars, 1620), are entirely convincing. One would very much like to know the relationship of Heywood and Rowley's play to *Pericles* (1606–8). There was undoubtedly a Stuart taste for exploiting the levels of the playhouse stage in nautical scenes, and I presume that the opening of *The Tempest* has the Master on the upper stage (quarterdeck) and the others on the platform (main deck). But these are secondary matters. The primary fact is always the platform, "the mainspring of Shakespeare's theatre", as J. L. Styan says.[9] It can look like the main deck of a ship, especially if one accepts the theory that the platform was not rectangular but tapered towards the audience.[10] How did Shakespeare exploit this aspect of its potential?

His later practice shows a cautious move towards the platform–ship analogue. Formally, the scene on Pompey's galley in *Antony and Cleopatra* (II. vii) has to count as a ship scene. In stage terms it is not projected as a nautical event, and it might be any interior scene until the revellers exit "down into the boat". The fact that it takes place on board ship is something we register intellectually but not viscerally. A true shipboard scene does not occur until *Pericles*. Gower's prologue to Act III ends:

> In your imagination hold
> This stage the ship, upon whose deck
> The sea-toss'd Pericles appears to speak.
>
> (ll. 58–60)

After which, *Enter Pericles, a-shipboard.* The physical resemblance of the platform to the ship's *deck* is very strongly asserted. The audience has been conveyed imaginatively *aboard* ship; it is not watching the ship from middle or near distance (as it is in Enobarbus's account of Cleopatra, or Chorus' evocation of Henry's fleet crossing the Channel). The transaction does, however, require the aid of the official mediator. No Gower, no shipboard scene. The fictive, the marvellous are brought into being by the stage magician. Finally, the opening of *The Tempest* is a *tour de force,* an invitation to the actors to lay on whatever is possible in the way of scenic or mimic marvels. Since it begins the play, it creates its own imaginative reality, from which we move to the land – and stay there.

It would seem from this brief listing that Shakespeare had a suspicion of, if not an aversion to, ship scenes. There is no instance at all before his late maturity, and a purely nominal one at that; that of *Pericles* requires a choric introduction; only at the last does Shakespeare's imagination freely operate on ship. And it might be thought, for example in *Antony and Cleopatra,* that Shakespeare had passed up some excellent opportunities for a shipboard scene. Facing the eternal choice of the playwright, show or tell, he chose to tell the battle of Actium. One can only guess at the reasons for this paucity of instance. It is conceivable that Shakespeare feared a kind of imaginative insecurity in his audience, when invited to put to sea. But the matter may be without great significance. As we have seen, there was no sixteenth-century vogue for ship scenes. Marlowe never wrote one, nor did Jonson. At all events, there are scarcely any opportunities in Shakespeare for the platform stage to act as ship's deck. It is the land that must supply analogues. And these are surely more various than has been realized. I offer here some instances in which the text, as it seems, is energized by the features of the platform stage.

III

Promontory first. In the supreme moment of *3 Henry VI* – it is Richard's soliloquy, placed in the very centre, that is both climax and definition to the play – the actor has this:

Why then, I do but dream of sovereignty,
Like one that stands upon a promontory
And spies a far-off shore where he would tread,
Wishing his foot were equal with his eye,
And chides the sea that sunders him from thence,
Saying, he'll lade it dry to have his way.

(III. ii. 134–39)

Promontory: "high land jutting out into the sea or lake" *(Oxford Paperback Dictionary).* That is not a bad description of the stage, thrusting in upon the audience. But observe the clarity and firmness of Shakespeare's composite image. The solitary actor, well downstage,[11] is the man on the *promontory.* (Conceivably, on one of the two corners available to him; this helps the "jut" sense.[12]) The audience is the *sea.* Richard, looking beyond the humanity from whom he is sundered, fastens his gaze upon some distant prospect that he will never attain. It is all there, in the starkness and resonance of the central image.

Hamlet touches the point glancingly. It is well known that at "this most excellent canopy, the air . . . this brave o'erhanging firmament, this majestical roof fretted with golden fire" (II. ii. 300–2), Hamlet will likely point to the stage canopy above his head, the "heavens". "This may have given special point to Hamlet's imagery here", as T. J. B. Spencer says.[13] It is not, I think, generally understood that the preceding phrase belongs to the same mental dimension: "And indeed it goes so heavily with my disposition that this goodly frame, the earth, seems to me a sterile promontory." *Sterile promontory* is one of Shakespeare's anticipatory or lead-in hints. The bare stage suggests the "sterile", and moreover Hamlet may well be close to the edge to bring out the force of "promontory". I take it that Rosencrantz and Guildenstern will be centre stage, while Hamlet wanders well forward; there must be a certain physical distancing between them, to contain Hamlet's alienation from his fellows, and also the digressive character of his long prose speech. A man on a headland is a man alone. "Promontory" here, then, is not central as in *3 Henry VI,* but sets up the clear theatrical allusion that immediately follows.

I do not, of course, claim that all references to "promontory" – there are eight in the canon – impart a special resonance, generated by the perceived resemblance of the stage to a promontory. The context must govern such matters, and most of the instances seem to me glancing and without special weight. It is, however, likely enough that when Prospero says "the strong-bas'd promontory / Have I made shake" (*The Tempest*, v. i. 46–7) he strikes his staff upon the floor. The phrase is in soliloquy, and is presumably delivered well forward; setting aside the general requirement of forward emphasis for the solitary speaker, Prospero needs to create space anyway for the impending group entrance of Ariel and company, which is to follow after line 57. He certainly has the staff in his hand, for he talks of breaking it in line 54. So it is inherently probable that a forward-stage Prospero, smiting the floor and making it resound, brings out the full force of "promontory".

And this same force, though not the identical word, is present in Titus Andronicus's great speech of woe. This not a soliloquy, but the central placing and emphasis of the similitude fix it in the audience's mind:

> For now I stand as one upon a rock
> Environ'd with a wilderness of sea,
> Who marks the waxing tide grow wave by wave,
> Expecting ever when some envious surge
> Will in his brinish bowels swallow him.
>
> (III. i. 93–7)

As clearly as in *3 Henry VI,* the image is controlled by its play-house context. The "waves" of the audience are those of the sea, the "rock" of Titus is the jut of stage on which he stands. (Conceivably, Titus's later "I am the sea" contains the meaning that the tears of the sea/audience are transferred to him.) That speech is there to be remembered, as Olivier's rendering is; and the Elizabethan audience would have additional reasons for remembering it.

To the same natural cluster of images belongs *cliff*. There are five references only in Shakespeare, of which two can be dismissed immediately as meaning "clef". Horatio has

> What if it tempt you toward the flood, my lord,
> Or to the dreadful summit of the cliff
> That beetles o'er his base into the sea.
>
> (*Hamlet,* i. iv. 69–71)

where *cliff* resonates only if we speculate on the use of the upper stage for the Ghost's appearance. That does not seem worth pursuing. We are left with *cliff* in *King Lear:* the Dover cliff is first mentioned by Gloucester (IV. i. 73), and it becomes the locale of the drama in IV, vi. And now the stage/cliff analogue makes everything work.

The scene is a virtuoso piece of dramatic writing, which is also a didactic exercise in the power of the imagination, aided by the arts of the stage, to overcome the facts of physical reality.[14] The dialectic is expressed in Gloucester's "When shall I come to th' top of that same hill? . . . Methinks the ground is even", and Edgar's replies "You do climb up it now. Look how we labour. . . . Horrible steep" (IV. vi. 1–3). Edgar must now lead Gloucester slowly across the level stage towards the front; and "Hark, do you hear the sea?" (l. 4) is charged with extra significance, for the *sea* is again the audience. Edgar's "murmuring surge" (l. 20) is the very sound of the playgoers, breaking in upon the mind of the blind man. He conducts Gloucester towards the edge of the stage until "Come on, sir, here's the place. Stand still" (l. 11). There follows Edgar's cadenza on the cliff, a chorus-like stimulus to the imagination, and

Gloucester	Set me where you stand.
Edgar	Give me your hand. You are now within a foot
	Of th'extreme verge. For all beneath the moon
	Would I not leap upright.

(IV. vi. 24–7)

I contend that Gloucester, at this point, is actually "within a foot" of the platform edge, "th'extreme verge". It is pointless to play the episode in mid-stage, where all can see that it is a harmless deceit.[15] What the stage knows about, what it has always revelled in, is *danger:* there must be a chance, one to draw the audience's soul out of its body, that Gloucester will fall off the cliff – and into the crowd. Similar accidents, planned or unwilled, have occurred all through stage history. So the blind man must tighten the audience's nerves at the platform edge. How Edgar accomplishes his trick may be endlessly debated. He might set Gloucester to face parallel with the line of the stage, or away from it. He might conduct Gloucester to the edge, then pull him back a little. What is desirable is that the audience should feel the presence of *cliff* (mentioned at line 67, "the crown o'th'cliff'"), and thus its emotional reality. A cliff is not something one looks at. It is something one falls off.

So far I have discussed passages where the stage metaphor ener-
gizes a moment in the drama. I now turn to the final metamorphosis
of the stage, which structures an entire play. The play is *The
Tempest*, and the metaphor is the island. Let us first establish the
linguistic facts. The family of *island* words *(isle, islander,* and so on*)*
has 77 references in the canon, of which 35 occur in *The Tempest*. The
main terms are *island* (18 references in *The Tempest,* out of 29 in the
canon) and *isle* (14 references, out of 40). Nearly half the canon's
allusions occur in one play. There is a strong and sustained
reminder that its action takes place on an island. After the initial
turmoil of the shipwreck, the drama subsides into Prospero's
autobiography; and that in turn rests upon "Here in this island we
arriv'd" (I. ii. 171). Here the play, too, stays.

Shakespeare exploits – he may have created – a metaphor which
Marvell later alluded to, in his poem on the same island:

> He lands us on a grassy Stage;
> Safe from the storm, and Prelat's rage.
> (*Bermudas,* 11–12)

In its inherent quality, the stage as island extends the idea of stage
as promontory. The stage/island, raised above its surroundings, is
lapped around by the audience/sea. *Island* has, moreover, the idea of
limitation, of confined and precarious territory which the sea
threatens to encroach upon. Though we are never given a clear
account of Prospero's island, it is evidently not large, and the sea is
never far away.[16] If Prospero's island is something more than an
atoll, it is something less than a spacious dominion. In its starkness,
its sense of limitation, and its atmosphere of encroachment, the
island offers deep likenesses to the bare stage on which the action
takes place.

The location is further marked by a decisive linguistic pointer,
the recurring use of "this". As we know, "this" is a strong word on
the Elizabethan stage, the more so given the declamatory and
emphatic style of Elizabethan acting.[17] The demonstrative pronoun
is often a stage direction, as for instance in Polonius's "Take this
from this, if this be otherwise." One must take seriously, then, the
coupling of "this" and "island". And the coupling is very frequent.

Of the 14 references to *isle,* 6 are preceded by *this;* the 17 references to *island* are on 10 occasions *this island.* I list a few instances, to illustrate their emphatic quality:

> I say by sorcery he got this isle . . .   (iii. ii. 51)

> This island's mine . . .   (i. ii. 333)

> I had peopled else
> This isle with Calibans   (i. ii. 352–3)

> Though this island seem to be desert   (ii. i. 37)

> Had I plantation of this isle, my lord   (ii. i. 145)

> Do that good mischief which may make this island
> Thine own for ever . . .   (iv. i. 217–18)

A vigorous and expressive gesture, most obviously an arm movement, would seem called for at each *this.* Moreover, "isle" and "island" are never words of general allusion. In *The Tempest* they are always specific; they refer always to the island of the play. *This isle* is the territory of the stage.

The stage territory is the cockpit of the actors. The best acting part in *The Tempest* is Prospero; the second best part is Caliban. When Caliban says "This island's mine" he disputes the overlordship with Prospero. Prospero, interestingly, never says that the island is "his"; he asserts only his right to govern. All Ariel wants is his freedom. It is a straight fight, then; and the dynamics of the action come down to the second actor's claim to *his* territory, the stage. He rallies his forces, and the primitive arithmetic of Trinculo's assessment contains the same idea: "The folly of this island! They say there's but five upon this isle; we are three of them. If th'other two be brain'd like us, the state totters" (iii. ii. 4–7). Three against two, a promising basis for revolution, or mutiny. Prospero's rule is always under threat, always in danger, as was the rule of Sir George Somers in the events that fired Shakespeare's imagination.[18] The plot against Alonso echoes the motif. The sense that the stage is there to be fought over is basic to the play.

The audience has the status of invisible denizen of the island. Shakespeare may, I think, have an effect in mind at

Adrian   The air breathes upon us here most sweetly.
Sebastian   As if it had lungs, and rotten ones.
Antonio   Or as 'twere perfum'd by a fen.

(II. i. 49–51)

The breath of the island air is that of the stage audience: the
metaphor and literal come together. Sebastian is, no doubt, of
Coriolanus's mind – "You common cry of curs, whose breath I hate
/ As reek o'th'rotten fens" (III. ii. 124–5) – and might well glance
backwards at the spectators, a couple of yards away, as he delivers
his line here. It is a stray connection with the audience. Another
such connection may be present during Iris's address to Ceres:

> thy broom-groves,
> Whose shadow the dismissed bachelor loves,
> Being lass-lorn; thy pole-clipt vineyard;
> And thy sea-marge, sterile and rocky-hard,
> Where thou thyself dost air – the queen o'th'sky,
> Whose wat'ry arch and messenger am I,
> Bids thee leave these, and with her sovereign grace,
> Here on this grass-plot, in this very place,
> To come and sport.

(IV. i. 66–74)

Shadow might be pointed at, as the natural product of the stage
overhang. ("Shadowe or cover" actually refers to the canopy, in the
Fortune's contract.[19]) If *pole-clipt* means "hedged in with poles", the
phrase indicates the area demarcated by pillars. *Sea-marge, sterile and
rocky-hard* is the final descendant of the promontory-rock effects I
have already discussed; the direction of Iris's gesture is an open
question. And *grass-plot* is the platform, especially its forward or
central portion. Such tactical moments emerge naturally from the
topography of the stage, and from the continuing island–stage
correspondence. Of an altogether different order are the hints
concerning the identity of the island.

Where is Prospero's island? The given geography has a
Mediterranean cast. The fauna is occasionally outlandish –
"wolves", "lions", "marmosets", "apes". The formation is "coral".
But these exotic pointers remain superficial. Underneath is a dense
body of suggestions that place the island much nearer home. Apes
and marmosets are outvoted by hedgehogs and moles. A. D. Nuttall

has nicely caught the quality of this play's nature poetry, and I cannot do better than quote his epitome:

> It, too, is full of minute observations and gigantic distances, with a strange salt-sweetness hardly to be found elsewhere. We may skim the play, creaming off images which illustrate its special flavour – 'the ooze of the salt deep . . . the veins of the earth when it is baked with frost', 'unwholesome fen . . . berries . . . brine-pits', 'yellow sands . . . the wild waves whist', 'sea-water . . . fresh brook mussels, withered roots and husks, wherein the acorn cradles', 'bogs, fens, flats', 'a rock by the sea-side', 'show thee a jay's nest and instruct thee how To snare the nimble marmoset; I'll bring thee To clust'ring filberts, and sometimes I'll get thee Young scamels from the rock', 'where crabs grow . . . pignuts', 'the quick freshes' – and the nature hymn at IV. i. 60ff., bristling with grain and grasses, wet with rain and dew. It is strange that this great nature poem is not better loved. It may be that the focus is too clear for our post-romantic eyes. Perhaps most of us would prefer 'showery April' to Shakespeare's more intimate, tactile 'spongy April'. This truthful clarity in the natural imagery, like the circumstantial elements in the plot, helps to draw from us that special credence, at once lively and in a state of suspense, which is proper to the play.[20]

Nuttall does not, however, go on to draw what seems to me the obvious conclusion: the island, for all its exotic touches, is conceived as English. This is no vulgarized Gauguin/Tahiti resort, but an earthy, damp, and strangely real territory, with a highly equivocal climate. Caliban (like Ferdinand) has to fetch in logs:

> He does make our fire,
> Fetch in our wood, and serves in offices
> That profit us.
>
> (I. ii. 313–15)

Not exactly a tropical paradise, this; one needs servants to make fires for precisely the same reasons one does in England. And following the standard Shakespearean technique, the explicit voicing of these hints is given to a clown:

> *Trinculo*   Were I in England now, as once I was
>
> (II. ii. 28)

"England" is always a strange and quirky resource for Shakespeare, one which changes its meaning from play to play. Here it is manifestly a laugh, and a peculiar frisson of alienation. But it can also make the connection that England is an island too, and that the production is taking place in it. The import of the larger connection passes beyond speculation. It strikes me as one of Shakespeare's characteristic dualities: one perspective shows us marvel, romance, wondrous scenic effects, the other insists that this play is no mere escapist fable. And it would be strange if, in the climactic play of the canon, Shakespeare were not to consider the matter of England.

If "the great globe itself" is seen as the reduction of England to a theatre, Prospero's melancholy leave-taking to the stage takes on an extra dimension of poignant meaning. The final phases of the play, however, return us insistently to the primary metaphor. Alonso recapitulates the action, in "who three hours since / Were wrack'd *upon this shore*" (v. i. 136–37), and Prospero repeats the reminder in

> know for certain
> That I am Prospero, and that very duke
> Which was thrust forth of Milan, who most strangely
> *Upon this shore,* where you were wrack'd, was landed,
> To be the lord on't.
>
> (v. i. 159–63)

The gesture must in each case mark the line separating stage from audience, *this shore* from the sea. The "vision of the island" (l. 178), Ferdinand and Miranda playing chess, is the discovery space, a great resource of the stage. That Miranda's "O brave new world / That has such people in't" embraces the whole house (and not just the stage audience) is at least plausible. But all works down to the apotheosis of the "poor isle" (l. 214), whose point is that it lacks the scenic splendours of the masque and any other kind of resource. The platform is itself alone.

At the end, Shakespeare definitively reorders the metaphoric relations of actor and audience. Prospero possesses a space defined by its bareness, and the solitariness of the actor who inhabits it:

> Let me not,
> Since I have my dukedom got
> And pardon'd the deceiver, dwell
> In *this bare island* by your spell.

The platform is now nothing more than the island, nothing but a parenthesis for human isolation. And the audience is the sea. But "No man is an *Iland,* entire of it selfe; every man is a peece of the *Continent,* a part of the *maine* . . . " The pursuant metaphor reaches out for society, and towards the help needed to reach the main:

> But release me from my bands
> With the help of your good hands
> Gentle breath of yours my sails
> Must fill, or else my project fails,
> Which was to please.

The actor-with-platform now becomes the ship, whose life and movement depend absolutely on the co-operation of larger forces. The splendid ambivalence of "breath" and "hands" once more finds a use. The metamorphosis of stage into ship carries with it the implication not only of departure but also of arrival.

2   *Richard III*: Bonding the Audience

The first thing that we know of *Richard III* is that it was a hit, and remained so. From the days of its mentions in Henslowe's diary and the five quartos by 1612, through the two centuries of Cibber's version, to the triumphs of Olivier's film and Guinness's opening night at Stratford, Ontario, *Richard III* has commanded popular success. Shakespeare seems to have expressed in it all that he knew of the means of controlling an audience: of creating, for the first time in his career, a star part, and of welding the audience into a fascinated and delighted unity. The relations between Richard and his audience are my subject.

I

The ground-plan of *Richard III* is that the audience supports the villain–hero, then abandons him. The formal action can be called the working of "retributive justice";[1] the audience experiences it as the waning of an affair, and a demonstration that actions will have consequences that include our emotional reactions to those consequences. Gloucester is in the first place a channel for the energies of the drama, impulses transmitted from stage to audience and back. Those energies are dark and primitive, emerging from a stratum of folklore and desire in the collective mind. Richard, clearly, permits the acting out of desires in the audience. He makes himself King; he takes his sexual rewards; he plans (but is unable to commit) incest. Against all the structures of morality, kinship, the needs of the tribe itself, the individual asserts himself. The process is made profoundly attractive, and in the end as profoundly repellent. The atavistic forces tapped by Richard are never far below the surface of the action. The folklore element suggests, for instance,

16

that Richard's status is that of Imposter. He is The Man Who
Would Be King, behind whom stretches a long line of tricksters.
Then, in the wooing of Lady Anne, we become conscious of another
myth: Beauty and the Beast. (It is a myth Middleton also exploits,
in *The Changeling*.) Nicholas Brooke finds echoes of de Sade in
Richard's treatment of Lady Anne. As Brooke remarks, the play's
"sexual current, prominent in this scene and equally so later in the
wooing of Queen Elizabeth for her daughter, is elsewhere frequently
felt, but very much as an undercurrent".[2] This is true, but it is
interesting that the sexual current is strong and explicit in Richard's
apotheosis, his address to the troops:

> You having lands, and blest with beauteous wives,
> They would restrain the one, distain the other . . .
> Shall these enjoy our lands? Lie with our wives?
> Ravish our daughters?
>
> (v. iii. 321–2, 336–7)

The appeal to the sexual and racial instincts of the soldiery, and the
proposition that the end of war is to get at the enemy's womenfolk,
can be looked at as a tactic of rhetoric: it can also be taken as a
straightforward exposition of Richard's psychology and values. The
soldiery/audience is appealed to at a certain level of the psyche. The
appeal is rejected, as it happens; but the intensity of the current is
fully registered.

From these hints of a dark pre-history to Richard, a shadowy
impression of his identity begins to emerge. That identity is,
however, based on an immediately available tradition. The great
container for Richard is the Vice-figure. The explicit reference does
not occur until III. i, but the Vice governs the frame of reference
within which Richard engages the audience. Richard alludes to a
network of devices, stratagems, traditions with which his audience
is well familiar. He can, for instance, be looked at as a mutation of
Herod in the mystery plays, a role "rooted in the tension and
interaction of the horrible and the comic".[3] The comic is the means
by which the audience both approaches the tyrant, and revenges
itself upon him. Richard, for his part, seeks to seduce the audience.
Audience rapport is the key to the early structuring of this play, and
we need to touch lightly on the obvious features of Richard's wooing
of his public.

(a)   *Soliloquies and Asides*

It is generally accepted that the soliloquies in *Richard III*, prior to the last one (v. iii), should be played as direct address to the audience.[4] The tone is ingratiating, and the audience flattered by being taken into Richard's confidence. We become accomplices. But these soliloquies cluster most densely around the early scenes, and they later fade. Thus the audience's regard for Richard is insidiously weakened. In the opening phase, Richard confides in us; in the second, in Buckingham; in the third, in no one.

The aside in *Richard III* is not really a miniature soliloquy, merely a joke that maintains good relations with the audience.

> (i)   Amen! And make me die a good old man!
> That is the butt-end of a mother's blessing;
> I marvel that her Grace did leave it out.
> (ii. ii. 109–11)

This aside presents Richard as Peck's Bad Boy, an endearing enough figure.

> (ii)   So wise so young, they say, do never live long.
> (iii. i. 79)

The aside is transmitted to Catesby and Buckingham, who illustrate a tactic of their master's:

> (iii)   *Catesby*   The princes both make high account of you –
> For they account his head upon the bridge.
> (iii. ii. 69–70)

> (iv)   *Hastings*   Nay, like enough, for I stay dinner there.
> *Buckingham*   And supper too, although thou know'st it not.
> (iii. ii. 121–2)

All instances of the aside occur in the first half of the play. Its lapse marks a weakening of the bond between Richard and audience.

(b) *Double Meanings*

The double meaning is a joke shared between Richard and the audience. While the remark is addressed to another character on stage, its import is clear and will be pointed up the actor. Thus:

(i)   We are not safe, Clarence, we are not safe.

                                                    (I. i. 70)

(ii)   Meantime, this deep disgrace in brotherhood
       Touches me deeper than you can imagine.

                                                    (I. i. 111–12)

(iii) I will deliver you, or else lie for you.

                                                    (I. i. 115)

(iv)   For they that were your enemies are his.

                                                    (I. i. 130)

(v)   Some tardy cripple bare the countermand.

                                                    (II. i. 90)

Buckingham is presumably the audience for whose benefit the last remark is passed; the others are all for the playhouse audience. Again, the pattern holds of an opening blaze of instances, soon extinguished. But while the immediate tactic lapses, the idea of double meaning broadens out into the superlative continuous jest of III. vii.

(c) *Wordplay*

Richard enjoys wordplay, usually of a rather obvious and mechanical type. The most advanced instance I can find is the reference to the "new-delivered Hastings" (I. i. 121), a neat hit at the innocent-babe aspect of Hastings. Otherwise Richard's wordplays do not test the powers of the audience:

(i)   Since every Jack became a gentleman,
       There's many a gentle person made a Jack.

                                                    (I. iii. 71–2)

(ii)   while great promotions
          Are daily given to ennoble those
          That scarce some two days since were worth a noble.
                                        (I. iii. 79–81)

(iii)   What, marry, may she? Marry with a king.
                                        (I. iii. 99)

These (with which one can include the oath-substitute of "Margaret") are broad and easy games with words, much in the Vice tradition and sure to win the approval of the audience. Shakespeare extends their use into the second half of the play, presumably because he finds them psychologically interesting. Richard, in the bad-news scene, has three in rapid succession:

(iv)   *Stanley*   Richmond is on the seas.
       King Richard   There let him sink, and be the seas on him!
                                        (IV. iv. 462–3)

(v)   *Stanley*   Unless for that, my liege, I cannot guess.
       King Richard   Unless for that he comes to be your liege,
                        You cannot guess wherefore the Welshman
                        comes.
                                        (IV. iv. 474–6)

(The word "liege" evidently touches a nerve: Richard had played on "true noble Prince" with Buckingham, IV. ii. 20.)

(v)   *Stanley*   No, my good lord, my friends are in the
                        north.
       King Richard   Cold friends to me! What do they in the
                        north,
                        When they should serve their sovereign in
                        the west?
                                        (IV. iv. 483–5)

The mind is trying to impose order on a dissolving world.

Wordplay is the crucial term for locating the traditions energized by Richard. It is focused to the clear exposition of

Gloucester	So wise so young, they say, do never live long.
Prince	What say you, uncle?
Gloucester	I say, without characters fame lives long.
	Thus, like the formal Vice, Iniquity.
	I moralize two meanings in one word.

(III. i. 79–83)

"Gloucester's reference to the 'formal vice, Iniquity' is – like Speed's – itself in the form of a pun, and it is a vicious and highly sophisticated kind of 'contrarie sence' in which Gloucester uses the verb 'moralize'."[5] Weimann marks the first and fourth lines in the passage cited as *aside*. That is the point, left open for performance, which characterizes the openness of the text to the traditional allusion. Richard may deliver the lines broadly, to the audience; or he may speak them covertly, to Buckingham. The one mode is the non-representational use of the *platea* (platform), a direct address to the audience. The other way assents to the realistic, *locus*-centred style. It is impossible and unnecessary to determine the matter; no doubt the actors' way of playing this passage (and others raising parallel problems) varied over the years in Shakespeare's lifetime. These options raise the question of the degree of obsolescence associated with the tradition. Weimann emphasizes the word "old" used of the Vice in *Twelfth Night* and *The Two Gentlemen of Verona*.

> These qualifications are, in Shakespeare, perhaps the most illuminating. The Vice was the *old* Vice, but *still* he could be used or referred to; and the words "old" and "still" indicate the dialectic of innovation and tradition by which Shakespeare's wordplay actually thrived upon the diminishing tensions of *mimesis* and ritual, matter and impertinency.[6]

The psychology of the role adapts easily to the dualism of the tradition. There is nothing improbable in the notion of a person modelling himself upon a stereotype of conduct, or using this stereotype as a point of departure. "And what's he then that says I play the villain?" demands Iago. It seems likely that the development of dramatic style was able to assimilate the traditional Vice. The villain/hero who takes the audience into his confidence – for whom an antecedent can be found as far back as the Chester Cycle[7] – is absorbed into the self-consciousness of Richard. Even at the very end, there is no contradiction between tradition and psychology. The demoniac energy of Richard,

> March on, join bravely, let us to it pell-mell;
> If not to heaven, then hand in hand to hell.
>   (v. ii. 312–13)

calling for a horse with his last breath, is simply the "terrible exuberance" of the Vice, riding off like Nichol Newfangle to hell.[8] On all counts, traditional, tactical and psychological, the Vice-material strengthens Richard's bond with the audience.

The Vice is a technical means of establishing rapport. It will not in itself guarantee success. Richard remains, a man. His links with the audience must consist of something other than jokes and direct appeals. Behind the tricks is a sensibility; and Shakespeare develops, in that sensibility, a sympathetic exploitation of class attitudes. One cannot adequately discuss the core of this play without reference to class.

II

Richard is an aristocrat. And some of his utterances assert an aristocrat's outlook, one founded on pride of family and class:

(i)   Unmanner'd dog, stand thou, when I command!
                                         (i. ii. 39)

(ii)   Ay, and much more; but I was born so high.
        Our aery buildeth in the cedar's top,
        And dallies with the wind and scorns the sun.
                                         (i. iii. 262–4)

(iii)   Madam, I have a touch of your condition,
        That cannot brook the accent of reproof.
                                         (iv. iv. 158–9)

But this is not his norm. The substantive mass of Richard's expression is not aristocratic, or is so only in a highly qualified sense. Richard habitually expresses himself in a mode that is highly accommodating to his audience, one that is in essence bourgeois.

Let us explore this class sensibility. Richard's imagery and turns of speech are often colloquial, and often suggest the attitudes of businessmen. Thus the "packhorse", "post horse" references, and "But yet I run before my horse to market" (I. i. 160); financial and monetary terms crop up: "then must I count my gains" (I. i. 162), "And yet go current from suspicion" (II. i. 95), and "Repair'd with double riches of content" (IV. iv. 319). Buckingham adjures him to act "Not as protector, steward, substitute, / Or lowly factor for another's gain" (III. vii. 133–4): Queen Margaret repeats the perception in

> Richard yet lives, hell's black intelligencer,
> Only reserv'd their factor to buy souls
> And send them thither;
> (IV. iv. 71–3)

A consistent strain of language suggests the concerns of a business-man. I do not conclude, as does Paul N. Siegel in his Marxist reading, that Shakespeare is drawing a blackly negative picture of bourgeois values and using it to establish Richard's evil.[9] The *dramatic* function of this bourgeois language is to maintain contact. It is in the main jocular, ingratiating, reaching to the concerns and awareness of the general audience. It is oddly reassuring, as though Richard were saying "I am really one of you, you know." Richard's is the language of the common man, rather than the *grand seigneur*.

Moreover, this linguistic quality reinforces certain class attitudes that the play on occasion calls upon. In I. iii, Richard seeks to unite his stage audience behind him, and against the Queen's kindred, the Woodvilles; and in this the stage audience is the model of the larger audience. "The world is grown so bad / That wrens make prey where eagles dare not perch" (I. iii. 69–70). For a moment there is a hallucinatory resemblance between Richard and Third Citizen, each crying Woe! on social dissolution. The hits at "jacks" and "nobles", already quoted, extend the point. At bottom Shakespeare traces a commonplace of history, the alliance between nobles and people. No positive values are imparted to the Wood-villes. There is nothing in stage terms to counter Richard's view of them. Thus the Woodvilles focus whatever class resentment is in the audience: they are jumped-up gentry, a category which by definition no one (noble, popular or bourgeois) cares for. So Richard succeeds in rallying the audience behind him.

Again, take Richard's relations with his subordinates. For most of the play he is affable enough, if with an edge. "How now, my hardy, stout, resolved mates! . . . I like you, lads, about your business straight" (I. iii. 339, 353). Richard's excellent relations with the Workers reaffirm the audience rapport: no side about Richard, one might say, a jovial and understanding employer of the old school. (Note how his word "business" conflates the suggestions of trade and stage.) Not till IV. iii do these master–servant relations appear repellent ("Kind Tyrrel", "gentle Tyrrel", which is altogether disgusting) and not till the last speech of all does Richard address Catesby as *slave,* a word that reveals all by reducing Catesby from a name to an object. In sum, Richard for most of the play seems the sort of aristocrat of whom the general audience could reasonably approve, a noble with the common touch.

And this common touch emerges most subtly, I think, in the attitudes which Richard constantly invokes, sometimes by way of proverb. These attitudes I characterize as citizen-morality. They are promoted (and, of course, subverted) by the very personae that Richard assumes: pious contemplative, unworldly innocent, country boy. All of them seem to me broadly bourgeois in origin, though I do not take the term literally, as applying to a town resident. Take the country boy: the persona Richard affects in I. ii – one unused to the traffickings of Court politics – sorts well with the rustic quality of some of his lines: "But yet I run before my horse to market" (I. i. 160), "He is franked up to fatting for his pains" (I. iii. 313), "Small herbs have grace, great weeds do grow apace" (II. iv. 13), "Short summers lightly have a forward spring" (III. i. 94), "A milksop, one that never in his life / Felt so much cold as over shoes in snow" (V. iii. 325–6). The "strawberries" episode suggests a man more at home in a garden than the Court, and "Chop off his head" is a woodman's phrase. Beyond the suggestions of milieu lie those of values. The wooing of Lady Anne is conducted by the Ardent Lover; nothing in Shakespeare is closer to the world of Colley Cibber, and the language of Richard here is eighteenth century, pure Drama of Sensibility. It illustrates a vein of popular morality and moralizing easily detectable elsewhere: "Now by St. Paul, that news is bad indeed! / O, he hath kept an evil diet long, / And overmuch consum'd his royal person" (I. i. 138–40), "God will revenge it" (II. i. 139), "O, do not *swear,* my Lord of Buckingham" (III. vii. 220 – Buckingham has just said "Zounds"). The marketing of the candidate to the citizenry is founded on the proposition that

Richard "is not an Edward! / He is not lulling on a lewd love-bed . . . Not dallying with a brace of courtesans" (III. vii. 71–74). No phrase sums up this aspect of Richard's appeal better than Buckingham's "I never look'd for better at his hands / After he once fell in with Mistress Shore" (III. v. 50–1). This is proto-Pecksniffianism, a homage to moralizing, bourgeois righteousness. A picture emerges from all this of a reformist Richard, clean of speech and living, dedicated to restoring the standards of civic morality that have so sadly lapsed during the reign of Edward the Lustful.

It is high comedy, reaching its zenith in III. vii. Just how much of an edge there was in the presentation, then guying of these bourgeois attitudes is hard to say. I suspect that the satirical bite may have been fiercer than is commonly imagined.[10] After all, the Vice tradition was rooted in challenge to the *status quo,* in a "moral scepticism" directed at the conventional pieties: "I pray thee, tel me what meneth this word charity? / Because thou does make it so holy."[11] Weimann suggests that the jingling language of the Vice may have recalled Lollard heresies;[12] and the "deep divines", who flank the Protector in the draft-Richard convention, may hark back to older traditons. It is not hard to see a vein of popular anti-clericalism touched on here.[13] One cannot dogmatize on such matters, but I propose a formulation of audience response along these lines: Richard and his accomplices promote a broad vein of citizen-morality attitudes which are presented in an engagingly comic light in the early scenes; they culminate in the high-pressure, satiric comedy of III. vii, which simultaneously delights and appals. Thereafter the mode changes. The comedy turns sour. (The formula is not so very different from *Romeo and Juliet.*) Proverbs are extensions of "they say", and in the end it turns out that "they" are right. Citizen-morality, like God, is not mocked for five acts.

In all this, the movement of audience response is governed by an ancient formula: "The Vice criticizes from the audience's point of view."[14] Richard reaches out towards the *platea:* he is the presenter, the commentator on the *locus* scene. His genial mockery of civic values, his command of proverbial lore, his mode of delivery, all create a special relationship with his audience. But that is for three acts. The Vice stands outside the action to begin with, and is then gradually sucked into it. The proverbs, jokes, wordplays die away. The audience becomes progressively more detached, then alienated. The Vice's ultimate dialogue (the v. iii soliloquy) is with himself, not the audience. The story of the last two acts is the turning of the audience against Richard. Much of this needs no comment; it is a simple revulsion against a monster. But I want to trace the lines of Shakespeare's technique in this matter. If class attitudes influence the bonding process in the early stages, the later stages rely on the imperatives of place. It is location, region, and ultimately nation that define the audience of *Richard III*.

III

No play of Shakespeare's is so strongly imbued with a sense of place, of national identity as the sum of many locations. Counting indifferently together names of places and titles (I shall come to the distinction later), I find some 50 English locations mentioned, whether of house (Crosby House), county (Devonshire) or city (Exeter). Of these 50, many are referred to on several occasions. The Tower of London is mentioned no fewer than 25 times. All the major regions of the country are covered. The cumulative effect is of a massive impregnation of the text with a sense of England, the full extent of the land.

The broad effect is one thing. The individual references are something else. For each single allusion to a place, there is a justification peculiar to drama: some member or members of the audience will know it, or have some connection there. Shakespeare must have learned early that the chances of striking a chord in a spectator's mind, through the allusion to some out-of-the-way place, are fairly high. Someone always turns out to have come from Haverfordwest. It is not unlike the well-known odds against finding two people with identical birthdays in a quite small group. And all London references must connect with virtually the entire audience. The effect of each reference is a minor shock of recognition. The place-names are tiny foci of dramatic energy, pellets of meaning released into the audience's bloodstream. "I used to live near Baynard's Castle." "You *can* stay at Stony Stratford, but I wouldn't, not with the inns there." "Curious how you always get good strawberries in Holborn." "My mother came from Hereford!" And so on. There is much dramatic energy stored away in these innocent namings.

If that were all, it would at least justify raising the matter. But Shakespeare does not deploy place-names on a scatter principle. He organizes these far-flung places into patterns which are, as I take it, the final index to his sense of the audience's identity.

In Act I, *Richard III* is above all a London play. Set in London, the milieu has great solidity of impression. The many references to the Tower, with all its associations, symbolize the dramatic centre of London; and we hear of Chertsey, St. Paul's, Crosby House, Whitefriars. The provinces exist only through the references to St Albans and Tewkesbury (and thus, the past of the Civil Wars). Titles aside, that is all. Through this phase the audience enjoys the greatest rapport with Richard. Broadly, then: in the first act we are Londoners in London, and we approve of Richard.

Act II begins the move away. Although the play is still set in London, the impress of topography is much weaker. The talk is of travel, of Ludlow, Stony Stratford, Northampton. It is an undular strategy, in which Shakespeare creates a psychic wave away from London.

Act III anchors itself very firmly in London. All the manoeuvrings take place there, and the citizenry must establish itself as belonging to the capital. Similarly with the Recorder, and the Lord Mayor of London. The Tower, of course, dominates all. The local allusions continue, and we are reminded of Holborn, the Crown, Baynard's Castle, Tower Bridge, St Paul's, Crosby House. The provinces (Pomfret, Hereford) are still at the margin of this play's consciousness. The general audience, at the height of its pleasure in Richard, is continually reminded: this is London, our city.

The peremptory "Stand all apart" (IV. ii. 1) announces the second part of the play. That order to the courtiers figures Richard's relations with the audience. From now on he is distrustful, paranoid; the old rapport is gone. The allusions to place impart the new reality. We have no sense of London, though the play is still set there. All the talk is of the provinces, which now come to the fore of the play's consciousness. The roll-call is impressive: Exeter, Brecknock, Salisbury, Devonshire, Kent, Yorkshire, Milford, Dorsetshire, Pembroke, Haverfordwest. The West, Wales, even Kent are in arms. The North (of the "cold friends") is the distrusted, hostage-enforced alliance with Derby. The drama, then, composes a map which we can discern without much difficulty: the great rough triangle of the British isle has arrows pointed, threateningly, towards London. And with them the psychology of the play changes. The provinces are right, and London is wrong.

With these harsh explicit indications come subliminal suggestions all tending to the same end. For we cannot confine our assessment of place-names to a simple symbolism of region and rebellion. We have to recognize the soft mutation of *place* to *title*. This play often broods on "title", as Brackenbury does – Richard, the Duchess of York, Queen Elizabeth all talk about it – and the union of place and name has its significance. We have largely lost our sense of it today, with our later traditions of title based on surname, or battle-honour, or simple euphony allied to tenuous local connection (Attlee, Alamein, Avon). It is salutary to be reminded, as one can still be in England today, that a local magnate counts for something in the area whose name he bears. Titles were based on the possession of land; they were not empty honorifics. A name signified a reality. Thus insidiously, the play makes its point along these lines: *Dorset* may be a cipher, but *Dorsetshire* (IV. iv. 522) matters. The titles, hence the land, are in arms against the King.

And who supports the King? The symbolism of Act v is clear. Only from the South East is there any support: the Duke of Norfolk, and the Earl of Surrey, his son. (The name of Richard's horse, "White Surrey", underlines the symbolism.) Outside the South East only Northumberland sides with Richard, and he is dubious, stigmatized as "melancholy" and having his comments repeated for Richard's benefit ("What said Northumberland as touching Richmond?"). Derby has already made his arrangements. The titles offer a diagram of forces here.

The conclusion is a boar-hunt, conducted in the middle of England.

> Thus far into the bowels of the land
> Have we march'd on without impediment; . . .
> The wretched, bloody, and usurping boar,
> That spoil'd your summer fields and fruitful vines,
> Swills your warm blood like wash, and makes his trough
> In your embowel'd bosoms, this foul swine
> Is now even in the centre of this isle,
> Near to the town of Leicester, as we learn.
>
> (v. ii. 3–4, 7–12)

Bosworth is almost the dead centre of the land. There the forces of the South and West, united with the symbolic representatives of London and the Midlands (Richmond and Oxford), defeat the tyrant, who is let down by the North and inadequately defended by his own South East. The land renews itself, gathering together to kill the usurper to its title. (Again, as in *King John,* Shakespeare plays on the synecdoche of "England" and "King of England".) The triumph of right is also the triumph of the provinces. The alienation of the London audience is now complete: it detaches itself from "the bloody dog"[15] and declares itself for the morality of the provinces, and thus the nation. Title (the Crown), land, people and audience unite. In the end, the bonding principle of the audience is that it is English.

3 *The Comedy of Errors*: the Subliminal Narrative

To see *The Comedy of Errors* as the first of the final romances is no great paradox of vision. It is true that commentators used always to stress the Plautine, and thus the farcical nature of the play. For most of them, *The Comedy of Errors* was in the first instance an adaptation of Plautus's *Menaechmi,* and one took it on from there. But the archaic and primitive elements of the play are now more visible than in the past. Northrop Frye points to its dark underside, "which brings the feeling of the play closer to the night world of Apuleius than to Plautus".[1] Such a perception makes the play more of a comedy, less of a farce. Moreover, the romances are now thought of as a vital and ultimately defining area of the canon, to an extent which would not have been conceded a generation ago; so there is a disposition to admit *The Comedy of Errors* as an anticipation, not merely an experiment. Manifestly, the play works towards the experience of reconciliation and discovered identity, anticipating the drift of the romances. That can be taken for granted. I want here to look at some ways in which this curiously layered play organizes our experience. The most helpful commentary on its provenance, for my purposes, is Anne Barton's:

> Behind the *Menaechmi,* as behind all the plays of Plautus, lay a Greek original now lost. Mistaken identity and the recovery of lost children seem to have been almost obsessive preoccupations of the New Comedy written by Menander and his contemporaries towards the end of the 4th century B.C. A response, probably, to the political chaos of a Hellenistic world that was filled with displaced persons, where children were often 'lost' by parents too poor or too distracted to cope with them at the time of their birth.[2]

If one substitutes "under" for "behind", the metaphor becomes more pointed. Under the Roman play is a Greek play; under the Greek play is an action so vaguely apprehensible as to merit only "pre-Hellenistic", the archetypal experience of wandering, loss and rediscovery. The lost Greek original silts down on to a folk memory. This has little to do with "sources", as conventionally understood.[3] *The Comedy of Errors* is a palimpsest, not of composition, but of experience.

I

Aegeon is the framing definition of the experience, and of its cultural pointers. He is the Wanderer. He tells of tempest, shipwreck, the parting of family, loss, quest:

> Five summers have I spent in furthest Greece,
> Roaming clean through the bounds of Asia.
> (I. i. 133–4)

Aegeon's account has diverse resonances, part literary, part pure folk memory. The immediate possibility is the parallel with Aeneas's wanderings. At the beginning of Aegeon's prolonged recital of woe comes

> A heavier task could not have been impos'd
> Than I to speak my griefs unspeakable:
> Yet, that the world may witness that my end
> Was wrought by nature, not by vile offence,
> I'll utter what my sorrow gives me leave.
> (I. i. 32–6)

First noted by Theobald, this seems an audible echo of Aeneas's address to Dido, and it is meant I think to be picked up. It is not simply that there is a repetition of situation – the ruler commands the wanderer to speak – and substance, Aegeon's first two lines corresponding to the general sense of Aeneas's

> infandum, regina, iubes renovare dolorem,
> Troianas ut opes et lamentibile regnum
> eruerint Danai, quaeque ipse miserrima vidi.
> (*Aeneid*, II. 3–5)[4]

It is rather that the whole expressive unit founds itself on "unspeakable: Yet . . . ", repeating the Virgilian device, in which, after a brief intermediary passage – one waits for the "sed" – it comes in

> sed si tantus amor casus cognoscere nostros
> et breviter Troiae supremum audire laborem,
> quamquam animus meminisse horret luctuque refugit,
> incipiam.
>
> (10–13)

and Book II is under way. "Infandum . . . sed . . . incipiam" translates closely into "Unspeakable: / Yet . . . I'll utter", and the authorities are satisfied that the imitation is conscious.[5] The basis for the scholarly consensus is research into the grammar school fondness for the first six books of the *Aeneid*, as much as the verbal parallels. I should myself hazard that Shakespeare is tapping a shared English experience of much of the audience, the acquaintance with certain books of the *Aeneid* at school. The incorrigible conservatism of the English grammar school is such that anyone studying Latin in the Fifth form today is likely enough to be reading Book II of the *Aeneid* – as Shakespeare, if he went to Stratford Grammar School, did.[6] At all events, we can think of the layer of reference here as Roman, or more accurately Latin.

Scholars like to deal with the Latin aspect, because it involves the objective certainties of Renaissance education and textbook adoption. The Greek aspect is much less stressed, because there is apparently much less there to stress. Jonson's (and Baldwin's) phrase, "Shakespeare's small Latine and less Greeke" says it all. Yet it is clear that Odyssean themes are strong in the romances.

> Both Homer and Shakespeare weave in a great deal of marvel, risk and triumphant adventures into their tales, use a plot about a wandering journey towards home filled with incidents of shipwreck and loss, stress a mingling of blessings and sorrows in the lives of their protagonists, and end their romances with a final reunion scene in which husband and wife, father and child, ruler and kingdom are reunited.[7]

From this angle alone it is reasonable to take Aegeon as "an early anticipation of this type of wandering figure".[8] In fact, a Homeric parallel surfaces in *The Comedy of Errors*, for there are passages that

hint broadly at Book XI of the *Odyssey*, and the transformation of the
mariners into animals. The idea is well launched in

Dromio S.	This is the fairy land; O spite of spites!
	We talk with goblins, owls and sprites:
	If we obey them not, this will ensue,
	They'll suck our breath or pinch us black and blue.
Luciana	Why prat'st thou to thyself and answer'st not?
	Dromio, thou drone, thou snail, thou slug, thou
	sot!
Dromio S.	I am transformed, master, am I not?
Antipholus S.	I think thou art in mind, and so am I.
Dromio S.	Nay, master, both in mind and in my shape.
Antipholus S.	Thou hast thine own form.
Dromio S.	No, I am an ape.
Luciana	If thou art chang'd to aught, 'tis to an ass.
Dromio S.	'Tis true; she rides me, and I long for grass.
	'Tis so, I am an ass.

(II. ii. 188–200)

The Odysseus figure, Aegeon in the opening scene, becomes by easy
transference Antipholus of Syracuse: "I'll stop mine ears against the
mermaid's song" (III. ii. 163). And the allusion is made formal by
the Duke, who exclaims "I think you all have drunk of Circe's
cup"(V. i. 270).[9] There is a running parallel between *The Comedy
of Errors* and the *Odyssey*. The *Aeneid* and the *Odyssey*, then, symbolize layers of experience here. The vertical structure of allusions is
a metaphor for the psychic layers to which the play appeals.

II

Roman on Greek: that is our code for the opening. The allusions,
conscious or subliminal, to the *Aeneid* and the *Odyssey* conduct us
into the play world. It is Hellenistic, archaic, romantic. "For
Shakespeare", says Bullough, "romance was mainly of the
Mediterranean."[10] The local associations of Ephesus would also
mean something to the Elizabethans. They thought of it as a great
seaport, renowned for its Temple of Diana. St Paul stayed there for
two years.[11] Hence the audience would connect it with St Paul's
Epistle to the Ephesians, and its appeals for domestic unity. They

would also remember that Ephesus was known for sorcerers and
exorcists, and for St Paul's "curious acts". The Biblical allusions
help to establish the dark underside of this play. But these cultural
referents are absorbed in the broad symbolism of the action and its
background, with the atavistic appeal to collective memories of
wandering and loss. Always at the back of the action is the sea, as
great a presence here as in *The Tempest*. It is the sea that parts
Aegeon and his family, that brings Antipholus of Syracuse to
Ephesus, that calls him throughout. "For he is bound to sea, and
stays but for it" (IV. i. 33). "Both wind and tide stays for this
gentleman" (IV. i. 46). That sense of the sea – waiting, pulling,
imperious – is strong in *The Comedy of Errors*. Not only is it a
reminder, in its ebb and flow, of the mysterious forces that govern
the individual, it is the image through which the individual defines
himself:

> *Antipholus S.*   I to the world am like a drop of water
> That in the ocean seeks another drop,
> Who, falling there to find his fellow forth,
> Unseen, inquisitive, confounds himself;
> So I, to find a mother and a brother,
> In quest of them, unhappy, lose myself.
>   (I. ii. 35–40)

> *Adriana*   For know, my love, as easy may'st thou fall
> A drop of water in the breaking gulf
> And take unmingled thence that drop again,
> Without addition or diminishing,
> As take from me thyself and not me too.
>   (II. ii. 124–8)

It is another version of the theatre experience, with the audience
(see Chapter 1) the sea. Both Antipholus and Adriana find in the
sea the deepest formulas for human identity. It is a symbol that
transcends cultural allusion.

   In fact, this play constantly reaches towards the universal. If
Measure for Measure is the most Freudian play in the canon, *The
Comedy of Errors* is the most Jungian. It is rooted in the collective
subconscious, and archetypes of enduring power are presented. The
plot itself is a playful rendering of the hostile brother motif, a theme
which as Aronson points out recurs often in Shakespeare.[12] Here,

the brothers are unwitting not hostile; it is only through ignorance that Antipholus of Syracuse intrudes upon his brother's domain. The Syracusan appears, archetypally, to be the "younger" brother; he is defensive, apprehensive, easily daunted (but luckier, for all that). His enduring impulse, when confronted with difficulties, is to take to the boats ("I long that we were safe and sound aboard", IV. iv. 150), while the "elder" brother is passionate, overbearing, a fighter. This mutuality of temperament is a part of the psychic integration of the play. Then again, Luciana provides perhaps the clearest statement in Shakespeare of the anima archetype.

Antopholus S.   It is thyself, mine own self's better part,
                  Mine eye's clear eye, my dear heart's dearer heart,
                  My food, my fortune, and my sweet hope's aim,
                  My sole earth's heaven, and my heaven's claim.
                                                    (III. ii. 61–4)

She, for Antipholus, is "the embodiment of this omnipresent and ageless image [of woman] which corresponds to the deepest reality in man".[13] The final transformation of the anima is the Abbess, who also combines the functions of Great Mother and Wise Old Man. In the end, the Syracuse merchant attains his "heaven's claim", too. The archetypes, to which I shall return later, are the inner substance of this drama. The archaic is simply the period costume of the universal.

III

Let us turn to the general experience of the opening scene. Its narrative is, as Northrop Frye says, "a sophisticated, if sympathetic treatment of a structural cliché".[14] The hieratic solemnity of the opening has the decorum of tragedy:

Aegeon   Proceed, Solinus, to procure my fall,
           And by the doom of death end woes and all.
                                         (I. i. 1–2)

The speaker – and thus, at this moment of supreme weight, the play – invites the Duke to define the experience as tragic. He, for 23 lines, appears to pronounce the verdict of tragedy. Yet there are

hints of unwillingness to complete the definition. "I am not partial
to infringe our laws" begins to sketch an apology; he explains at
length that the Syracusans and Ephesans have similar edicts; he
indicates that a heavy fine would suffice, but that Aegeon's property
is only a tenth part. He draws the only available conclusion,
"*Therefore by law* thou art condemn'd to die." The Law says, in
effect, "what else can we do?" It is not the brutal imposition of iron
statute that the more literal-minded commentators imagine. So,
when Aegeon hopelessly acquiesces,

> Yet this my comfort; when your words are done,
> My woes end likewise with the evening sun.
>
> (26–7)

the Duke, somewhat uneasily, invites Aegeon to keep the conversation going; something might turn up.

> Well, Syracusan, say in brief the cause
> Why thou departed'st from thy native home,
> And for what cause thou cam'st to Ephesus.
>
> (28–30)

The play now changes, for all its dramatic energies are concentrated upon Aegeon. The prisoner transforms the court. As narrator, he takes over; he holds the audience in a spell. It is a display
of magic, the power of the story-teller. In performance it is not to
be sabotaged by the director.[15] Length here is not tedium, but
the evocation of a primitive experience, the submission of an audience to the teller's capacity to create a world (cf. Sheherezade).
Its immediate consequence is a shift in roles for Aegeon and the
Duke. Prisoner and judge become story-teller and audience; hence
Solinus becomes a suppliant:

> *Do me the favour* to dilate at full
> What have befall'n of them and thee till now.
>
> (122–3)

His next speech is openly apologetic, "Now trust me, were it not
against our laws . . . My soul should sue as advocate for thee"(142,
145). The power of the teller has already wrought against the
framing definition, tragedy. There are hints in the main narrative,
too: "happy but for me, / And by me, had not our hap been

bad . . . Was carried towards Corinth, as we thought . . . By fisher-
men of Corinth, as we thought" (37–8, 87, 111). The actor is
entitled to glean some laughs from the repeated "as we thought": he
is obeying the larger instructions of the script, and "as we thought"
is a pointer towards the whole.[16] Having proposed itself as tragedy,
the play converts into an intimation and promise of comedy. The
narrator, defying the logic of *therefore by law,* wills the marvellous,
the death-suspended, the comic, and the audience assents to the
logic. The "law" will yield to a yet stronger force.

   This force manifests itself through fantasy. *The Comedy of Errors* is
organized along two lines of psychic advance. One is that of erotic
promise, unbelievable good fortune, discovered identity, the fulfilment of all one's desires. The other is that of loss, shattered identity,
pain. The first line is stronger, and its triumph never really in
doubt. The second is always present, often uppermost, at all times
shadowing the experience of cast and audience. Threat and promise
make up the fantasies of this play, and we ought to catch at their
blurred shapes.

IV

Antipholus of Syracuse has the largest speaking part, and channels
much of the play's experience. His character-note is longing, a
yearning for fulfilment in relationship; and the refused dinner-
invitation leads to

> Farewell till then. I will go lose myself,
> And wander up and down to view the city.
> (I. ii. 30–1)

For him the action is compounded of vague threats:

> They say this town is full of cozenage,
> As, nimble jugglers that deceive the eye,
> Dark-working sorcerers that change the mind,
> Soul-killing witches that deform the body,
> Disguised cheaters, prating mountebanks,
> And many such-like liberties of sin.
> (I. ii. 97–102)

and allure:

> To me she speaks; she moves me for her theme.
> What, was I married to her in my dream?
> Or sleep I now and think I hear all this?
> What error drives our eyes and ears amiss?
> Until I know this sure uncertainty,
> I'll entertain the offer'd fallacy.
>
> (II. ii. 180–5)

The fear, be it noted, is of *foreigners*. The archetypal challenge to self comes from strangers. Equally, the invitation comes from the exotic, the alluringly strange. So, through the curtain of doubts:

> *Dromio S.*   This is the fairy land. O spite of spites!
> We talk with goblins, owls, and sprites:
>
> (II. ii. 188–9)

and his own confusions:

> *Antipholus S.*   Am I in earth, in heaven, or in hell?
> Sleeping or waking, mad or well-advis'd?
>
> (II. ii. 211–12)

Antipholus goes into the house:

> I'll say as they say, and persever so,
> And in this mist at all adventures go.
>
> (II. ii. 214–15)

The echoes are of a fairy world. There is the house, there is the fair witch, offering whatever inducement of gingerbread or blandishment that can tempt the hero – or victim. Antipholus, a little o'erparted with the hero-role, quakes: but enters.

The play now enters (III. i.) upon its most intense and symbolically resonant phase, for it becomes the experience of Antipholus of Ephesus, shut out from his own home. The situation is enduringly fascinating: modern folklore abounds with tales of people who slip out of their apartment for a moment, usually in *déshabillé*, and find themselves locked out with alarming consequences. No doubt some of the anecdotes are true, but the market is larger than the instances. Antipholus of Ephesus, rooted in the reality of his calling and on his home territory, sees the world transformed. The familiar marks crumble. Moreover, behind the obvious shock of exclusion, there is a profoundly disturbing sexual threat, one which commentators habitually ignore.

Act III, scene i, as all agree, is based on Plautus's *Amphitruo*. It was a popular grammar school text, and Baldwin thinks that Shakespeare read the Latin original in the fourth form.[17] In the Plautine original, Amphitrion is shut out of his house, while Jupiter makes love to his wife Alcmena. Plautus dramatizes a primal fear. And a section of Shakespeare's audience would recognize the Plautine source. But the remainder of the audience would in any case receive the impression of sexual congress behind locked doors, which the play creates in its own right. The previous scene has ended on a note most favourable for Antipholus of Syracuse: Adriana is clearly in a mood to charm her husband, and is insistent that they are *not* to be disturbed:

> Come, sir, to dinner. Dromio, keep the gate.
> Husband, I'll dine above with you today
> And shrive you of a thousand idle pranks.
> Sirrah, if any ask you for your master,
> Say he dines forth and let no creature enter.
> Come, sister. Dromio, play the porter well.
>
> (II. ii. 205–10)

The audience is now to be teased with a sexual fantasy.

It is confirmed in the heavy verbal underlining of III. i. There's an easy bawdry in

Dromio E.   Let my master in, Luce.
Luce   Faith, no; he comes too late . . .
Dromio E.   Have at you with a proverb: Shall I set in my staff?
                                          (49, 51)[18]

If Antipholus of Ephesus does not realize the appalling implications of his "Are you there, wife? You might have come before" (63), the Elizabethan audience will help him out. Dromio adds to the effect with "Your cake here is warm within" (71), "cake" being "woman",[19] and his next line, "It would make a man mad as a buck to be so bought and sold" presents his master as a male deer in rutting season, and a cuckold. The worst, so the audience is led to

suppose, has happened. Antipholus thinks it too, and evidently
plans a sexual revenge with the co-operation of the Courtesan:

> I know a wench of excellent discourse,
> Pretty and witty, wild, and yet, too, gentle,
> There will we dine. This woman that I mean,
> My wife – but, I protest, without desert –
> Hath oftentimes upbraided me withal.
> To her will we for dinner . . .
> Since mine own doors refuse to entertain me,
> I'll knock elsewhere, to see if they'll disdain me.
>   (109–14, 120–1)

"Knocking" is standard slang for sexual entry.[20] But above all, the
double-entendres and bawdry of the text stem from the stage
symbolism itself: the house, perceived from earliest times as the
coding for woman, and the knocking at the gates, the male attempts
at entry. The symbolism is the more charged if the nature of the
inner action is considered. What is held before the audience as a
theatrical possibility is incest.

Incest takes up some space in the canon. The remarriage of
Gertrude to Claudius is held to be incestuous, and the charge is
repeated in Hamlet's final words to Claudius ("thou incestuous,
damnèd Dane"). Father–daughter incest appears in *Pericles*.
Though not named by Henry, the "incest" of his marriage to his
brother's widow is the core of the discussion in *Henry VIII*, II. iv. The
word is a metaphor for the relations of Isabella and Claudio ("Is't
not a kind of incest, to take life / From thine own sister's shame",
Measure for Measure, III. i. 138–9), and a type of hypocrisy for Lear:
"thou simular of virtue / That art incestuous" (*King Lear*, III. ii.
54–5). Lucrece has "Guilty of incest, that abomination" (*The Rape
of Lucrece*, 921). Richard III plans to marry his niece. If one takes
the canon as a giant exploration of human consciousness, incest, in
several of its variant forms, is more than a marginal presence in that
consciousness. Here in III. i, at the midpoint of *The Comedy of
Errors*,[21] incest is the compelling fantasy which is held before the
audience as a likely reality. It is the dark centre of a play shot with
fitful visions. Has it happened?

No, it has not. Act III, scene ii, takes the audience away from the
vertiginous edge, and conducts it towards sanity and order. It
rapidly becomes clear that the encounter between Adriana and

Antipholus of Syracuse has been a fiasco. Luciana's first line tells all: "And may it be that you have quite forgot / A husband's office?" which is plain enough speaking. Luciana upbraids Antipholus for the disastrous dinner-party – here as earlier the play anticipates *Macbeth* – and Antipholus confirms matters with "Your weeping sister is no wife of mine" (42), by which time, if not earlier, the audience must be aware that Shakespeare has been trifling shamelessly with its sensibilities. The play now modulates into mere comic dalliance with incest, for Luciana believes herself to be courted by her brother-in-law (which we know not to be true). A final tease is to come, for the actress is entitled to garner all she can from Adriana's "Which of you two did dine with me today?" (v. i. 369). But that is Shakespeare the professional milking a situation dry. The real message, which is one of reassurance, has come earlier through numerous channels. And here we should pause to take in one of them, the suggestions that link the action with England.

v

There is no doubt of the archaic character of this play. But it overstates matters to assert that "Shakespeare draws away from everything that is local or specialized in the drama of his day."[22] A residue of dramatic material obstinately insists that *The Comedy of Errors* is played before an English audience around 1590. The inn references are clear enough; theatregoers know and love hostelries. The "Centaur" and "Tiger" have not yet been located, but the "Phoenix", thrice mentioned, was the sign of a London tavern and of a shop in Lombard Street. It is referred to in the prologue of Jonson's *The Staple of News*.[23] The "Porpentine", mentioned five times, was the name of a Bankside inn; "Shakespeare's audience probably knew it well."[24] The inn references function as psychic stabilizers. Then, money. This play has no truck with drachmas. *Guilders* it is for the Second Merchant and for Solinus, who also speaks of *marks*. *Marks* touches off some wry levity with the Dromios. The coinage of the last two acts is *ducats*. It appears that "Many foreign coins were in continual circulation in England during Elizabeth's reign",[25] hence the coinage has a distinctly English, as well as Continental, reference. I do not know a more infallibly precise index to the nature of reality, throughout the canon, than money; and these guilders, marks and ducats figure the idea of the *foreign at home* which is basic to this play. They circulate happily with the honest *sixpence,* which turns up in the hand of Dromio of Ephesus. His brother takes charge of *angels.* And *gold,* of course, is much with us here: "universal, immutable, impartial" as de Gaulle observed. It is the true international currency of the mind.

Dromio's tour of modern Europe, focused on the symbolic geography of fat Nell (III. ii), extends the audience's reassurance that all will be well. The theatrical point about topical references is that only a home-grown audience can get them. Whatever the precise meaning of "France . . . arm'd and reverted, making war against her heir" (III. ii. 122–4), the mental dimension of the passage is contemporary Europe, centred on England. Similarly, one makes jokes about Irish bogs and Scots barrenness from England. The comic lewdness of the passage defines its general import, a signal that the play is going to pull out of its baffling and vestigially frightening confusions.

England signifies reassurance. And this subliminal message has been sent even at the shock of III. i, the moment when Antipholus of Syracuse discovers that his own door is locked. Dromio, obeying his master's orders, shouts "Maud, Bridget, Marian, Cicely, Gillian, Ginn!" (31). Suddenly Roman, Greek, Biblical, Mediterranean cease to bear upon the dramatic experience. After all, we are back home. It is impossible to take seriously a setback in which we are excluded from Bridget and Maud. Typically of *The Comedy of Errors,* its playing with primal anxieties is accompanied by signals of primal comfort.

VI

Even so, the later phases of *The Comedy of Errors* handle archetypes of serious and compelling authority. Much of Act IV is spun out of purgatory, or hell.

> *Dromio S.*   No, he's in Tartar limbo, worse than hell,
> A devil in an everlasting garment hath him . . .
> One that before the judgment carries poor souls to hell.

(IV. ii. 32–3, 40)

Antipholus's "chain" (51) is in the logic of association the bondage of hell. There are hints of "redemption" (IV. ii. 46), and "Paradise"

(IV. iii. 16), but the prevailing state is captivity, with "prison", "sergeant" and "durance" the guiding terms. Deliverance is the ship, "the bark Expedition put forth tonight" (IV. iii. 37), which Antipholus of Syracuse, as in a dream, is unable to reach. Instead comes the Courtesan, "Mistress Satan . . . the devil's dam" (IV. iii. 48–50), to frighten Dromio of Syracuse. Hell, however comically rendered, is the motif of Act IV. It is a nightmare, a bondage from which the captive actors struggle to be free.

Hence, in the symbolic logic of the drama, *hell* modulates into *devil* and then into *possession*, which in turn yields to a ritual of exorcisement:

> *Dr Pinch*   I charge thee, Satan, hous'd within this man,
> To yield possession to my holy prayers
> And to thy state of darkness hie thee straight!
> I conjure thee by all the saints in heaven!
>   (IV. iv. 54–7)

Hell having been redefined as *possession*, the way is open for Act V's line of strategic advance. Exorcisement gives way to convalescence. Adriana sees the process purely as recovery, "And bear him home for his recovery" (V. i. 41), but the Abbess invests it with religious associations:

> How long hath this possession held the man?
> . . . he took this place for sanctuary,
> And it shall privilege him from your hands
> Till I have brought him to his wits again,
> Or lose my labour in assaying it . . .
> . . . I will not let him stir,
> Till I have us'd the approved means I have,
> With wholesome syrups, drugs, and holy prayers,
> To make of him a formal man again.
>   (v. i. 44, 94–7, 102–5)

A ritual of healing is envisaged. The Priory, before whose gates the final action takes place, is the *sanctuary* of body and mind, the guarantor of the values of the close.

But these values are not achieved without an episode of significant turbulence. The cruel and anarchic spirit of comedy, now operating through Antipholus of Ephesus, breaks out of bondage and expresses a myth of liberation. It comes in two versions, the servant-messenger's:

> My master and his man are both broke loose,
> Beaten the maids a-row, and bound the doctor,
> Whose beard they have sing'd off with brands of fire;
> And ever, as it blaz'd, they threw on him
> Great pails of puddled mire to quench the hair.
> My master preaches patience to him, and the while
> His man with scissors nicks him like a fool.
>
> (v. i. 169–77)

and Antipholus's:

> Along with them
> They brought one Pinch, a hungry lean-fac'd villain,
> A mere anatomy, a mountebank,
> A threadbare juggler and a fortune-teller,
> A needy, hollow-ey'd, sharp looking wretch,
> A living dead man. This pernicious slave,
> Forsooth, took on him as a conjurer,
> And gazing in mine eyes, feeling my pulse,
> And with no face, as 'twere, outfacing me,
> Cries out, I was possess'd. Then all together
> They fell upon me, bound me, bore me thence
> And in a dark and dankish vault at home
> There left me and my man, both bound together,
> Till, gnawing with my teeth my bonds in sunder,
> I gain'd my freedom, and immediately
> Ran hither to your Grace:
>
> (v. i. 237–52)

The violence of this episode is evidently designed to release the emotional tensions created by the action. Liberation, we note, is accompanied by revenge: Antipholus of Ephesus goes in for outright torture of Dr Pinch, a feature he naturally omits from his report. That is why Shakespeare needs to plant two versions. In this most binary of plays, there are always two sides to events: what it looks like, and what it feels like. The messenger reports two dangerous lunatics on the rampage; Antipholus of Ephesus gives us the other side, the experience of hellish incarceration (in the "vault at home")

with the "living dead man", a kind of zombie,[26] as the guardian of
the underworld. *Freedom* becomes a plea to (and for) *Grace*. And, in
the play's terms, grace is bestowed.

It takes on the form of a rebirth:

> Thirty-three years have I but gone in travail
> Of you, my sons, and till this present hour
> My heavy burden ne'er delivered.
>
> (v. i. 400–2)

says the Abbess, making the entire action the convulsions of
delivery. The symbolism is confirmed in the lines which follow:

> The Duke, my husband, and my children both,
> And you the calendars of their nativity,
> Go to a gossips' feast, and go with me;
> After so long grief, such nativity!
>
> (403–6)

As Alexander Leggatt notes, "the final image of security is not a
wedding dance but a christening feast, a *family* celebration".[27] With
the *naming* of characters comes the affirmation of identity, family,
society (for the Duke presides, as he should). The dark coupling at
the centre of the play has led to a rebirth of the family, a restatement
of relationship. And in keeping with the standard Shakespearean
technique, the frankest statement of the implications is given to a
clown:

> *Dromio S.*   She now shall be my sister, not my wife.
>
> (416)

The prohibition on incest is the foundation of the family. That, and
the graceful settlement of the primogeniture issue, marks the
decorous conclusion to the play. What the Dromios exit into, what
the audience is left with, is *home*.[28]

4 Discomfort in *The Merchant of Venice*

The central experience of *The Merchant of Venice* is no doubt concentrated into the Trial scene, and the defeat of Shylock. I take the comment of Heine's English playgoer to be exemplary: "the poor man is wronged!"[1] That is to say, the audience will experience emotional turbulence, charged with its particular sense of the rights and wrongs of the encounter, but tending always towards the assertion that this is *not right*. The mind rejects the outcome. Now this will be so whatever the shifts of performance values, for *The Merchant of Venice* has the self-adjusting elasticity of the great play. I assume that Shakespeare's intention was to build into the text a strategy for confronting the audience with its own assumptions and wishes. "Here is a murderous Jewish usurer, defeated by Christian legal skill. Are you happy about it?" However primitive the audience, however gross its anti-semitism, the fate of Shylock would always challenge it. But the play works for different audiences, that know much more, and for different actors. Laurence Olivier, in Jonathan Miller's production at the National Theatre (1970), made Shylock a deeply sympathetic figure. He became a Jewish financier, blackballed by the Gentile business community, in whom rejection had turned rancour into a cancer. The pain of Shylock's exit, and the (literally) hair-raising howl off-stage that followed it, will never be forgotten by its audience. Bassanio, who with a swift gesture silenced Gratiano's gloating, spoke for the audience's shame. Yet Olivier's Shylock is not the only way for a modern audience, and it was quite unlike Patrick Stewart's for the Royal Shakespeare Company (1978). The actor has since acknowledged that he found the part extraordinarily taxing to prepare for, and he managed it on the formula: "Shylock is a despicable human being, who is also a Jew." Stewart's Shylock made no obvious appeal for sympathy: a hard, embittered man, he struck his daughter, was out to get

Antonio by all means under the law, and at the end – so far from collapsing – simply made his peace with the Venetians. His unspoken thought was "If that's what they want, so be it." This Shylock would survive. The audience's feeling of fascinated revulsion was, I think, general.

I don't want to sketch in a stage history of *The Merchant of Venice* here, but merely to illustrate the main, and obvious point: this is a deeply disturbing, unpleasant play, which succeeds in being disturbing and unpleasant under entirely different circumstances of history, audience response, audience understanding of anti-semitism, and actors' approach. It is not a play rendered obsolete by history. And it gives evidence of its vitality by its capacity to offend. It is, as Laurence Danson observes, "the only one of Shakespeare's plays . . . which a sizeable body of sane people might consider unfit to be seen or read".[2] He cites a *New York Times* editorial (31 March 1974) arguing "Why Shylock Should Not Be Censored". That reaction is most interesting, and it is far from unique. The RSC, for instance, has been urged of recent years not to perform *The Merchant of Venice*. Everyone agrees that it is a great play. Few like it, and many find it repugnant. Myself, I should prefer to acquiesce in the logic of the text, and say: the disturbed reaction is the correct one. We recognize the play through its attack upon us. The grand object of *The Merchant of Venice* is to create feelings of unease, disturbance, insecurity, perhaps guilt, revulsion, repugnance – in a word, and to simplify, discomfort.

Now much of the foundation for this discomfort is well known, and has been extensively analysed. There is the ambiguity of the play's title, for instance, a masked question posed openly by Portia: "Which is the merchant here, and which the Jew?" (iv. i. 172). Graham Midgley has convincingly argued that the play sets up a constant balancing and comparison of Shylock and Antonio. Throughout, the opposition between Christian/Venetian and Jewish values is examined with an underlying scepticism. One need not go all the way with A. D. Moody's judgement, "the play does not so much celebrate the Christian virtues as expose their absence",[3] to agree on the ironic, probing quality of this play's intelligence. The Venetian characteristics are certainly etched in with something other than affection. So "law", "justice", "mercy", for instance, are subject to a dramatic analysis that goes far to erode their claimed meaning; and the debate on "usury" focuses much of this tendency, for the notion that taking interest was abominable was in 1596 drifting out on the tide of history. But I propose here to take for granted the general intellectual tendency of *The Merchant of Venice,* which is to challenge conventional attitudes towards the chosen counters of discourse. I want to get at the play on another tack, the way in which the audience's sensibilities are manipulated by the social transactions depicted on stage. This is a play that treats often of social tensions, most clearly in the framing scenes, first and last, and I want to bring out these indications into the open. Small enough in themselves, they are a system of nuances that adds up to a pattern of discomfort, a communal subtext that is in the end a figure for the audience's unease.

I

The opening scene affords an anthology of social discomforts. This is the first play in the canon to utilize the mid-scene opening ("Nay, but this dotage of our general's / O'erflows the measure") and Antonio enters, continuing a conversation he already finds tedious. "In sooth, I know not why I am so sad" suggests that he is repeating the disclaimer. The opening impulse of the play is to resist an enquiry felt to be irksome:

> It wearies me; you say it wearies you;
> But how I caught it, found it, or came by it,
> What stuff 'tis made of, whereof it is born,
> I am to learn;
> And such a want-wit sadness makes of me,
> That I have much ado to know myself.
>
> (I. i. 2–7)

More than that, the speech is controlled by courtesy. That is the initial coding of the discomfort, a situation felt to be embarrassing held in check by the social disciplines.

Then follows the inquisition by Salerio and Solanio. The stage dynamics are based on number, two to one: they interrogate Antonio, taking it in turns. There is a needling, probing quality to the dialogue. The investigators want to find out the cause of the malaise, and they will not accept evasions. The audience's mind is concentrated upon Antonio (not the other two) and partakes of his wish to escape the enquiry. As for the possibilities raised by

Salerio and Solanio, the subject matter is itself ominous, fearful. The talk is of shipwreck and loss, and how intensely worried they would be. Underlying this is a deeper cause of embarrassment for Antonio. They do not understand. The vulgar worldliness of their speculations has no bearing upon his state of mind. They seek to define angst in terms of banal anxieties.

Salerio and Solanio, then, are company that is spectacularly irksome. Their attempts to probe Antonio degenerate into "Why, then you are in love" (46). In the light of the play as a whole – there is not the slightest reference to a link between Antonio and any woman – Solanio's suggestion is oafish. He gets nowhere with it. The first 60 lines of the play contain only two speeches by Antonio (totalling 12 lines), and he is clearly sitting the problem out. Silence is the only defence.

There is in fact a certain atmosphere here. Antonio has made his point, in the only way he can, and even Salerio and Solanio are beginning to get it. When Bassanio and company enter, Solanio immediately takes his chance to escape, a sure sign of relief:

> Here comes Bassanio, your most noble kinsman,
> Gratiano and Lorenzo. Fare ye well:
> We leave you now with better company.
>
> (57–9)

A touch of asperity here, in "better company"; also "your most noble kinsman" exploits the ambiguity of the superlative, i.e. the phrase means "very noble" or "the most noble you've got". How do we read Salerio's excuse, "I would have stay'd till I had made you merry, / If worthier friends had not prevented me" (60–1)? Perhaps, as John Russell Brown suggests, he and Solanio see themselves as taking on a quasi-medical function, talking Antonio out of his melancholy.[4] Perhaps they are being sensitive, perhaps insensitive; one never knows. Perhaps their main drift is to subscribe to the Venetian code-word, "merry" (even the bond is "a merry sport"): so Antonio falls short of an important social norm. ("Joviality," Graham Greene has remarked, "that's what's wrong with England, joviality.") At all events, the gulf between Antonio and his companions widens. And they are as glad to go as he is to see the back of them.

Something of this comes out in the badinage of the changeover. Antonio has what comes perilously close to a discourtesy, a very firm verbal push to his friends:

> Your worth is very dear in my regard.
> I take it, your own business calls on you
> And you embrace th'occasion to depart.
>
> (62–4)

One might say that Antonio is finding, with the utmost politeness, a reassuring formula for his friends' departure. But they take it amiss. Bassanio's greeting to them is

> Good signiors both, when shall we laugh? Say, when?
> You grow exceeding strange: must it be so?
>
> (66–7)

Evidently, a grimace has passed between the outgoing and incoming set. "He's being – difficult" is the unstated message. And now the newcomers fall to the work of social rehabilitation.

The situation of repressed embarrassment recurs with new variations. To begin with, Antonio must endure a phase of that exquisite social agony, during which one must wait for other people to depart before one can speak to the object of desire alone. Lorenzo realizes this well enough ("We two will leave you", 70), but Gratiano fails to take the hint. Not only does he stay and talk – agony enough, in all conscience – but with a sure instinct for the wrong choice of topic, he raises the very subject that opens the play.

> You look not well, Signior Antonio;
> You have too much respect upon the world:
> They lose it that do buy it with much care:
> Believe me, you are marvellously chang'd.
>
> (73–6)

Is there anything more profoundly irritating than to be told, by successive acquaintances, "You're not looking well today", followed by the same (wrong) diagnosis of one's complaint? Gratiano (whose name, as all concur, conveys *grate*) launches after Antonio's brief parry into a prolonged cadenza on himself, "Let *me* play the fool" (79–104). It is length as tedium, a device Shakespeare was to use often. But even then, Gratiano has not finished. Shakespeare finds for him another of his deadly touches: he is the man who announces his intention to depart, and then – stays. After "Fare ye well awhile: / I'll end my exhortation after dinner" (103–4),

Lorenzo shepherds him towards the door with "Well, we will leave you then till dinner-time": Gratiano speaks two more lines of witless joviality, which contain no hint of departure, then Antonio applies the closure with "Farewell: *I'll* grow a talker for this gear" (110). Two more lines, good only for editors to write notes on, and the exit of Gratiano is accomplished. At last Antonio and Bassanio are alone.

This is relief, of a sort, and it expresses itself in the odd line (found in Q and F) that editors have puzzled over, Antonio's "It is that anything now" (133). As I read it, the line needs no emendation. Its incoherence is its point. The surge of relief in Antonio finds its outlet in a vague collocation of words, not an ordered statement. The relief, however, is momentary only, for Bassanio and Antonio enter upon a new phase of embarrassment. Bassanio is in the position of having to ask an important favour, not for the first time. The ensuing conversation is decidedly sticky. The main contours here are not in doubt, but I point out the twin technical means through which Shakespeare fixes the dialogue: the verse/prose, and you/thou switch.

The general conversation has been in verse, from the play's beginning. Following Antonio's unintelligible "It is that anything now", Bassanio speaks in prose: "Gratiano speaks an infinite deal of nothing, more than any man in all Venice", and so on (114–18). That is a distinct change of tone, a move towards a more informal, intimate style of conversation. It is proper for close friends who are now alone together, and moreover Bassanio's purposes would be suited by the more intimate style. But Antonio resists it. He raises the matter that has been on his mind, in verse:

> Well, tell me now what lady is the same
> To whom you swore a secret pilgrimage,
> That you today promis'd to tell me of?
> (119–21)

Obviously, the subject matter as worded suggests a covert reproach. Formally though the speech is a declined invitation. Bassanio has proposed that they relax into prose, and Antonio has insisted on a degree of distance between them. This is to be blank verse occasion. Bassanio takes the point immediately, and launches into his preamble, in verse: "'Tis not unknown to you, Antonio" (122 ff.). What follows is a lofty exchange on "love", "owe" and "fortune".

The two enact, a little stiffly, the roles of Suppliant Friend and Generous Patron. There is a distance between them still, and it is identified in the persistent use of "you". I adopt here Randolph Quirk's formula of "The modern linguistic concept of contrast operating through *marked* and *unmarked* members . . . *You* is usually the stylistically unmarked form: it is not so much 'polite' as 'not impolite'; it is not so much 'formal' as 'not informal'."[5] Not until the final speech of the scene does Antonio reach towards his friend, with that word that signifies diminished mental distance, even physical contact, between them: "Thou know'st that all my fortunes are at sea" (177). The gap between Antonio and Bassanio is now closed. But the moment concludes a dialogue marked by reserve and unexpressed tensions.

I have laboured the social points in this scene, because it is always of cardinal importance to grasp Shakespeare's game from the start. His strategy is to set up a series of situations, that convey different modes of social unease. Now little of this need appear in performance. The dialogue is governed by a continuous courtesy, and only a first-class ensemble is in a position to bring out these tensions. One can say that the stage directions are all in the words. And I think that is always true. It might be more accurate to suggest that the *context* for the stage directions is in the words. The mass of signals in a Shakespeare text does not, at all points, coerce the actors into a fixed and circumscribed meaning. Those signals do, however, direct them to interpret the text within a certain field of force, a certain sense of impulses, inhibitions and provocations that have to be rendered into significant action. Whatever the actors make of it, the field of force of scene i seems to me clearly identified. It is one of tension, discomfort, and an inability to locate or resolve a problem.

II

Just as scene i makes its motto-statement for the play, the openings of several early scenes impart an identity and direction to the dramatic energies. Extended quotation is unnecessary here, and I cite the leading indicators. "By my troth, Nerissa, my little body is aweary of this great world" (i. ii. 1–2) translates angst into ennui, an undefined malaise into a more recognizable boredom. The scene's end is a threat from an unwelcome, black wooer, Morocco.

He, in turn, opens II. i, with "Mislike me not for my complexion", thus imparting his own sense of unease. Act I, scene iii, is a sustained embarrassment for Antonio and Bassanio, as they seek a loan from Shylock. Act II, scene ii, opens with a comic variant, Launcelot's psychomachia: "Certainly my conscience will serve me to run from this Jew my master" (II. ii. 1–2), and he debates the decision to change jobs. The third scene of Act II is dominated by Jessica's unhappiness, and she opens the scene with

> I am sorry thou wilt leave my father so:
> Our house is hell, and thou, a merry devil,
> Didst rob it of some taste of tediousness.
>   (II. iii. 1–3)

There is a consistent pattern here, of impulses that (however transmuted into comic or melodramatic modes) take as their point of departure a mood of unease. They blend, naturally, with the developing story of the drama, which is the reported bad news of Antonio's ships. But these dramatic impulses are not tied to the mere mechanism of plot and shipwreck. They are generated by the major dramatis personae, and the situations in which they continually find themselves.

Of Antonio, enough has been said here. His problem is at the core of the play, and however one interprets "I am a tainted wether of the flock, / Meetest for death" (IV. i. 114–15), it is as close as he comes to self-awareness. His presence always imparts a vague melancholia, a psychic disturbance to the company. But more needs to be said about Bassanio. To an extraordinary extent, he is entrusted with the task of carrying the unease of scene i throughout the play.

Bassanio's pattern, those unremitting collisions of circumstance and reaction by which we know a man's inner being, declares itself in embarrassment and shame. He is constantly faced with situations that embarrass him, and he as constantly escapes from them into situations that compel a further embarrassment. Bassanio is embarrassed in I. i when he has to ask his friend, yet again, for a large unsecured loan. He is embarrassed in I. iii when he has to humble himself before the appalling Shylock and prepare the ground for Antonio's loan. (The strain comes out in the nervous eagerness to get a quick answer from Shylock: "May you stead me? will you pleasure me? shall I know your answer?" I. iii. 7–8) He is embarrassed when Antonio accepts the Jew's bond, "You shall not seal to such a bond for me! / I'll rather dwell in my necessity" (151–2), but he lets Antonio do it for all that. He is embarrassed at being accompanied to Belmont by his friend and follower Gratiano, "lest through thy wild behaviour / I be misconst'red in the place I go to / And lose my hopes" (ii. ii. 178–80), but he lets him come. He would: Bassanio never deals with a problem by saying no.

The embarrassments do not end in Belmont. He has to tell Portia how much he has engaged himself to Antonio:

> and yet, dear lady,
> Rating myself as nothing, you shall see
> How much I was a braggart. When I told you
> My state was nothing, I should then have told you
> That I was worse than nothing; for, indeed,
> I have engag'd myself to a dear friend,
> Engag'd my friend to his mere enemy,
> To feed my means.
>
> (iii. ii. 256–63)

One can see that Bassanio's addiction to the simple truth is the cause – as it is the relief – of his embarrassments. Just as Antonio bailed him out before, Portia does now, with the offer of a handsome overpayment to Shylock. The Trial renews the problems, however. Bassanio is ashamed that he cannot save his friend from Shylock, and his protestation is singularly unconvincing:

> Good cheer, Antonio! What, man, courage yet!
> The Jew shall have my flesh, blood, bones and all,
> Ere thou shalt lose for me one drop of blood.
>
> (iv. i. 111–13)

He is ashamed to be taken up on his offer to the advocate, and to have to refuse Bellario the ring. He is ashamed when Antonio presses him to let Bellario have the ring. He is ashamed to tell Portia that he has parted with it: "I was beset with shame and courtesy" (v. i. 217). He was; he always is. The discomfiture of Bassanio is the core joke of the final scene, just as it is a recurring motif in the preceding play. Bassanio goes through *The Merchant of Venice* manfully mastering a silent squirm. His charm, social address and truthfulness place always the responsibility for relieving his distress upon others; which they do. Bassanio is a finished portrait (head and shoulders, shall we say, not full length) in a particular gallery which always interested Shakespeare, that dedicated to winners. Bassanio belongs to the group that contains Bolingbroke, Henry V and Octavius, whose fascinating blend of deficiencies and strengths brings them to the apparent edge of failure – and then, with an inner gyroscopic stability, back towards success. Bassanio succeeds by revealing his problems, and exporting them.

Enough of Bassanio. He treads a delicate social path, and its hairline risks bring out the finest qualities of others. His relationship with Portia is one of refined judgement of distance, and I do not wish to elaborate upon it here. It is however germane to my thesis to emphasize the quality of control that Portia exercises. This is a great lady, accommodating herself to the heterodox social problems of Nerissa's engagement (about which she has *not* been consulted), a trio of wooers, two of them totally unsuitable, the lumpish manners of Gratiano, the swarm of hangers-on that Bassanio has picked up and who hopefully deposit themselves upon Belmont. Since all this is an opportunity for the actress to play the grande dame, one usually misses the strain on stage: what one sees is a triumphantly successful actress in the prime of her career, exercising a magnetic and aristocratic dominance over a docile cast. What the text reveals is something more challenging. Portia's mastery is achieved over real social resistance. There is, for instance, in Act III, scene ii the moment of recovered gaucherie when Bassanio welcomes Lorenzo, Jessica and Salerio. They arrive at an apt moment, one which saves Portia the need to respond to Gratiano's graceless jest on "stake down", which by implicating his hostess in a sexual contest goes much too far. Bassanio's immediate reaction – possibly he feels the need to cover up for Gratiano's gaffe – is to welcome the new arrivals: "Lorenzo and Salerio, welcome hither". Then he realizes his own mistake; it is not his business to welcome the guests first. His reaction is swift:

> If that the youth of my new int'rest here
> Have power to bid you welcome.

Clearly, Bassanio glances at Portia at this point, and the look on her face is something lacking in warmth, for he hurries on to elaborate the excuse:

> By your leave,
> I bid my very friends and countrymen,
> Sweet Portia, welcome.
>
> (III. ii. 220–4)

The "sweet Portia" is a nicely ingratiating touch. It's up to the actress to decide how much edge she will put into the reply "So do I, my lord, / They are entirely welcome" (224–5). The point, however, is easily detectable. Note the chill in "*They* are entirely welcome", not "*You* are entirely welcome", and there is no follow-up address of welcome by Portia to the newcomers. The implication is: "You haven't taken over my household *yet*. Please make your friends welcome; and do not forget that I am châtelaine here." The passage is over a moment. It is another index of the unease that inhabits the transactions of this play. And in the end, the unease seems to be located, more than anywhere else, around the person who of all the major figures says least: Jessica.

III

There are three Jews in *The Merchant of Venice,* and I have least to say about the most important. We can pass over here the inner rage of Shylock, that quality of hate which can be nothing other than profoundly disturbing since its aim is to *kill,* at any cost to itself. Such a passion of destruction can only raise questions, like spreading ripples, in the society that has harboured it. Tubal, for our immediate purposes, is more interesting, because he is a normal member of Shylock's own community. Tubal is a sketch for a Jewish chorus. As Raymond Westwell has lately demonstrated (RSC, 1978), the actor playing Tubal can impart a sense of deep reservation about Shylock. The Jewish community withholds its approval. Tubal has been commissioned to carry out a specific task, to report on Jessica's doings in Genoa. He does so, but without comment on the rights and wrongs of the matter. His silence, as so many in this play, breeds meanings.

What emerges from Tubal's report to Shylock (III. i) is the curious structural parallelism between this scene and the opening. Shylock is being needled, as Antonio was. The stimuli take the form not of questions, but of fragments of information. Tubal, curious to see how Shylock will take it all, plays on his nerves by alternating the current, switching from good news to bad. It is a dialogue largely of single sentences, and the principle of alternation is marked. Tubal speaks first of his failure to find Jessica (bad) and immediately after of Antonio's ill luck (good). He reverts to Jessica's heavy spending in Genoa; then he swings back to Venice, "There came divers of Antonio's creditors in my company to Venice, that swear he cannot choose but break" (106–8). A paroxysm of joy from Shylock, then "One of them showed me a ring that he had of your daughter for a monkey" (111–12). Torture. "But Antonio is certainly undone" (117). I detect an implied hostility, if not subdued sadism, in Tubal's playing on Shylock's responses. It is, as I take it, Shakespeare's way of suggesting that the Venetian Jews have their own thoughts about Shylock. There is community, but not (I think) much friendship here.

Still, Jessica is the problem that Shylock bequeaths to Venetian Christian society, and the play. She is, in her way, a much more subtle and disturbing problem. Shylock, after all, is a monster. One can put up psychological and real fences around him. Jessica is a virtuous and attractive young woman, who voluntarily joins the Christian community and stands ready to be assimilated. She is not assimilated.

The Jessica of the central and late scenes we see only in Portia's household, and it follows that our sense of her new status is governed by her relations with Portia. And these are marked, on Portia's side, by an icy courtesy that projects a very strong sense of distance and distaste. The central point to grasp is that Portia *never*, at any time, volunteers a remark to Jessica alone. Her initial welcome, which I have already touched on, is to Lorenzo, Jessica and Salerio in company. During the discussion of Antonio's difficulties, Jessica volunteers a seven-line speech on her father's hatred ("When I was with him I have heard him swear", III, ii. 284–90) and Portia effectively ignores her by addressing her next remark to Bassanio, "Is it your dear friend that is thus in trouble?" (291) That is Jessica's single contribution to the conversation. In Act III, scene iv, Portia makes the arrangements to operate during her absence, and her instructions to Lorenzo convey her wishes with steely tact. Lorenzo is to be in charge, and

> My people do already know my mind,
> And will acknowledge you and Jessica
> In place of Lord Bassanio and myself.
>   (III. iv. 37–9)

Her "fare you well" is to them both: Jessica offers a humble "I wish your ladyship all heart's content", and receives the cool reciprocity of "I thank you for your wish, and am well pleas'd / To wish it back on you: fare you well, Jessica"(42–4). Portia's final words are a dismissal, not a parting wish – it is Jessica and Lorenzo who *exeunt*, leaving the châtelaine with Balthasar. And that is the sum of Portia's Act III conduct towards Jessica. For her part, Jessica stands in awe of Portia's patrician manner: hence she answers Lorenzo's query, "How dost thou like the Lord Bassanio's wife?" with a panegyric,

> Past all expressing. It is very meet
> The Lord Bassanio live an upright life;
> For, having such a blessing in his lady,
> He finds the joys of heaven here on earth;
>
> (III. v. 70–3)

One could expect nothing else. But Jessica's stated view of the matter is not a final judgement on Portia. It is simply half of a relationship of domination and subordination, of distance-in-proximity.

Act V is no different. Portia has nothing to say to Jessica, save this:

> Go in, Nerissa;
> Give order to my servants that they take
> No note at all of our being absent hence;
> Nor you, Lorenzo; Jessica, nor you.
>
> (v. i. 118–21)

An afterthought, phrased as a parallel to Lorenzo's prohibition, and a negative one at that! Scarcely the conversational material from which warm relationships develop. At the play's end, the good news about Shylock's deed of gift is assigned by Portia to Nerissa:

> *Portia*　　　　How now, Lorenzo!
> 　　　　My clerk hath some good comforts for you too.
> *Nerissa*　Ay, and I'll give them him without a fee.
> 　　　　There do I give to you and Jessica,
> 　　　　From the rich Jew, a special deed of gift,
> 　　　　After his death, of all he dies possess'd of.
>
> (v. i. 288–93)

Let us be fair: there is a real social and human problem. Jessica's relationship to Shylock means that he cannot openly be discussed, and there is only a single reference to the "rich Jew" in Act v. Jessica comes to represent the unmentionable. Still, the chill that marks Portia's conduct to Jessica is at variance with the warmth that, on occasion, she knows how to impart. One can reasonably conclude that Jessica has a long way to go in Christian society. She is a source of negative vibrations, a dead area with which the usual social impulses fail to connect.

That, one might say, is a generalized alienation, a young Jewess in a Christian society. Surely her husband is different? With Lorenzo there is a relationship of a different order? I do not think so: I believe that Shakespeare plants doubts even about Lorenzo-with-Jessica. The playful allusions to betrayal that open Act v have, of course, been recognized often enough. But what do they mean, and what are the lovers saying to each other?

Act v opens with what Peter Hall used to call "the Shakespeare music", a passage of such poetic beauty that the wits of the audience are naturally stilled. "The moon shines bright" says Lorenzo in line one, and the audience immediately relaxes; no one can *think* while the moon is shining. Let us consider the dark side of the moon, as the conversation develops.

Lorenzo   in such a night
           Troilus methinks mounted the Troyan walls
           And sigh'd his soul toward the Grecian tents,
           Where Cressid lay that night.
                                                    (v. i. 3–6)

A teasing reference to a man betrayed by his lover: nothing to it, of course, mere love-play. Only it has happened before. Lorenzo has spent a portion of Act iii, scene v in raising and continuing the jest that Launcelot is cuckolding him with Jessica: "I shall grow jealous of you shortly, Launcelot, if you thus get my wife into corners" (iii. v, 27–8). Ho, ho, indeed. But pattern is character, and Shakespeare takes the opportunity to sketch in a man interested in the topic of betrayal.

Jessica   In such a night
           Did Thisbe fearfully o'ertrip the dew

> And saw the lion's shadow ere himself
> And ran dismay'd away.
>
> (6–9)

As I read it, Jessica deflects the thrust by turning the dialogue into a more comic vein. It is not clear whether the reference is to Chaucer's *Legend of Fair Women:* I think it more natural to assume that the allusion is to Shakespeare's own recent work, *A Midsummer Night's Dream.* The suggestion in "And ran dismay'd away" is in any case mildly comic.

> *Lorenzo*   In such a night
> Stood Dido with a willow in her hand
> Upon the wild sea banks and waft her love
> To come again to Carthage.
>
> (9–12)

This love-tap is more serious. Aeneas was not betrayed by Dido; he abandoned her. Lorenzo fails to accept the invitation of the comic vein. He stays in the mode of tragedy, with the covert threat of abandonment. Here again is the needling quality we have noted earlier.

> *Jessica*   In such a night
> Medea gathered the enchanted herbs
> That did renew old Aeson.
>
> (12–14)

Jessica gives up the attempt to play it for comedy, and answers seriously and directly. The Medea-Aeson allusion is what I should term an "adjacent" allusion: Jessica refers not so much to what Medea did for her father – that would be pointless here – but for her lover, Jason. Jason is a name already known in this play (I. i. 172), and the meaning of Jessica's counter is obvious. She is saying: "Let me remind you that Medea betrayed her father for her lover, and so did I for you." And within this Chinese box of allusions is the bitter awareness that Medea was betrayed by Jason.

> *Lorenzo*   In such a night
> Did Jessica steal from the wealthy Jew

And with an unthrift love did run from Venice
As far as Belmont.

(14–17)

The core of meaning is in the change of mode. Lorenzo breaks off
the engagement. He senses the covert reproach in the Medea
allusion, and he moves from the obliquities of classical reference to
direct statement, in which his own debt is acknowledged. "Very
true: and you did run away with me, for love." He concedes her
case. So Jessica is allowed to make an open, and therefore more
harmless, reproach:

In such a night
Did young Lorenzo swear he lov'd her well,
Stealing her soul with many vows of faith
And ne'er a true one.

(17–20)

Lorenzo (who has provoked it all) forgives her the slander, and all is
well. The moon has come out again. But the dark clouds were there
a moment earlier, for all that.

Jessica becomes a focus of stillness and darkness. She says
nothing at all after the final entrance of Portia, and no one addresses
her, in 220 lines. So her last words are "I am never merry when I
hear sweet music" (v. i. 69). She is alien, unassimilated into the
Christian revelry. There is no reason why the audience should take
any notice of her, unless the director wishes it.[6] She is on the fringes
of the reunion, forgotten. But the total play is, after all, more than
any audience can assimilate or director register. In all the meanings
generated by *The Merchant of Venice,* Jessica's silence is the representative of the undefined, incurable malaise that haunts the action.
She is the dark fringe on the final scene which, in so much critical
and theatrical folklore, is a paean to harmony, reconciliation and
intimations of celestial accords.[7]

And it is nothing of the sort. Impression, of course, is in
performance everything, and few productions project anything but
a sustained glow here. The main theatrical purpose of Act v is to
exorcise Shylock: agreed. But the critic is not obliged to endorse
without reservation the cumulative history of performance. The text
continues to disclose its dissonances, and the total system of signs
points to a darker comedy than the theatre admits to. Consider the

substance of the dialogue: the Great Elizabethan Cuckold Joke. After its allusive initiation in the early lines, the joke is given main billing thereafter. Portia, no less, threatens it; Nerissa, naturally, follows her; and Gratiano, whose function it is to blurt out things no other Venetian would state openly, says "What, are we cuckolds ere we have deserv'd it?" One begins to wonder if the Venice of this play is not, after all, kin to *Othello*. Then there is Bassanio's relations with Portia. This is Shakespeare's first major experiment in comedy with female domination – the line of development culminates in Rosalind three years later – and we can, I think, assume a certain queasiness in at least the original audience here. Bassanio, the adventurer of Act I, becomes the subdued husband of Act V. There is no surer sign of personal uncertainty than variation in mode of address, and in the final scene Bassanio, incredibly, addresses Portia in six different ways: "Madam", "sweet Portia", "sweet lady", "good lady", "Portia", "sweet Doctor". That is the measure of Bassanio's unease, as it is the measure of Portia's patrician dominance.

It is that dominance, poise founded on great wealth, that holds together the gathering. Without it, the stage community would be revealed for the generally ill-ordered affair it is. Antonio, "I am th'unhappy subject of these quarrels" (V. i. 238), continues to shed his melancholia upon all who touch him. Bassanio, still embarrassed, subsides into the glow of his formidable partner. The alien Jessica, ignored, must submit to whatever icy courtesy is accorded to her as Lorenzo's wife. It would be tactless to let the imagination dwell on Lorenzo's future, while he waits for Shylock to die off. (Tenure as Portia's estate manager, perhaps, or is he to be set up in business?) Gratiano remains, as grating as ever, and this time receives the rebuke – "Speak not so grossly" (266) – he had so richly deserved earlier. He pays no attention, and the play, which had begun with malaise, ends with the most vulgar and offensive of all the jokes even Gratiano can muster.[8] This is the society that Portia presides over, and while she is speaking it seems controlled. We have returned to the formula of the opening scene, a situation of some tensions held in check by the social disciplines. But it is a precarious order. The final scene is the apotheosis of *The Merchant of Venice*. It is unease made concrete, unease made society. Nobody speaks of Shylock, and nobody speaks to his daughter.

5 *Twelfth Night:* the Experience of the Audience

Let the claret which Shakespeare drank, as we know, on expense account[1] symbolize the general experience of *Twelfth Night*. The taste of this play has the same tension between sweetness and dryness, which translates easily into the indulgent reveries of the opening and the realities of rain, ageing and work, in Feste's final song. To analyse this tension is surely the business of criticism. The experience of *Twelfth Night* blends our sense of the title metaphor with the growing magnitude of the joke that goes too far, and with it our grasp of the relations between the gulling and romantic actions. It is a matter of changing expectations, of a modified sense of the initial *données* of the play. *Twelfth Night* is played out, as it were, on a metaphysical revolving stage, which slowly rotates through half a revolution: the profiles that were presented to us at the beginning are not those of the end. The heads remain the same, the presented view is much altered. In the end the audience is asked to revise its judgement, not simply of people, but of a convention, "festive" comedy itself. And that is bound to be disturbing.

I

Let us sketch in the initial experience of an audience not closely acquainted with the text. *Twelfth Night* is advertised and known as a comedy; the audience expects to be amused and entertained. At once it encounters a romantic and lovesick Duke. In the second scene an attractive young lady emerges from a shipwreck, and determines to enter the Duke's service. We can see the future there clearly enough. In scene iii we meet the comics, Sir Toby Belch and Sir Andrew Aguecheek: why, this is the best fooling, when all is done. The form is now clear. A romantic main action, with some comic relief from a bibulous knight, two varieties of fool, and an intolerable bureaucrat who is obviously to be done down. We have it. The play can run on metalled lines into the future.

And for some time yet, there is no need to rethink this position. The revels of Act II, scene iii will secure the sympathy of the audience, and the great confrontation between Sir Toby and Malvolio does at the time seem like the life-force challenging the powers of repression and sterility: "Dost thou think, because thou art virtuous, there shall be no more cakes and ale?" As presented, there is no chance of an audience denying this affirmation. (Or critic, one might add. There is an all but universal convention for commentators to stand up and be counted as in favour of cakes and ale.) And if *Twelfth Night* stopped at Act II, scene iii, there would be no need to modify C. L. Barber's view of the matter. "The festive spirit shows up the kill-joy vanity of Malvolio's decorum. The steward shows his limits when he calls misrule 'this uncivil rule' . . . Sir Toby uses misrule to show up a careerist."[2] But that verdict is slowly phased out by the play itself. Not at first: the garden scene is pure delight. Here we yield absolutely to the pleasure of the gulling. One has to stress the point, for in the later stages the ultimate theatrical effect of guilt requires that we should have participated fully in the garden scene. There is a certain moral responsibility, even culpability, which the audience assumes in *Twelfth Night*: I don't think the play can be understood without it.

The scene in which Malvolio makes a fool of himself before Olivia (Act III, scene iv) begins to insinuate unease into the audience's consciousness. It is a scene we have been prepared for, and kept waiting for, and it is an unholy delight; yet the thought is emerging that Malvolio has committed an irretrievable *bêtise*. The activities of Sir Toby, Fabian and Maria begin to look like open sadism, and we may make the subliminal connection between Malvolio and bear-baiting, mentioned earlier (I. iii. 92; II. v. 8). Sir Toby's "Come, we'll have him in a dark room and bound" contributes to the unease, and so does its continuation:

> My niece is already in the belief that he's mad. We may carry it thus, for our pleasure and his penance, till our very pastime, tir'd out of breath, prompt us to have mercy on him; at which time we will bring the device to the bar and crown thee for a finder of madmen.
>
> (III. iv. 138–43)

The inexorable line of development holds into the cell scene of IV. ii, and however this is played, the audience is now conscious that the affair is much less funny than it was. The joke has been taken too far, and we know it. Let us hold on to that formulation, and cast back to the beginning of the play. The entire construct prepares us for our realization in the later stages. (One cannot point to a precise moment in Act III, or even IV, when the audience must become aware of its own queasiness, but it must surely happen.) The hints start, of course, with the title. Twelfth Night is a festival that has already been going on too long. Twelve days and nights of overeating and overdrinking, little or nothing done in the way of useful work; the Elizabethans were not so different from ourselves. By 6 January they were ready enough for one more party, and then back to work. The experience of satiety is confirmed in Orsino's opening words. They stem from a condition, "*If* music be the food of love, play on" that itself indicates an uncertainty about the festive mood. The terms that follow are *excess, surfeiting, appetite may sicken and so die, Enough, no more, 'Tis not so sweet now as it was before.*

This last is the motto-statement, and it should stand not only before the play as a whole but before Act II, scene iii. This scene, more than any other, evokes the experience of Twelfth Night. That is because it is a revel, which goes on too long, and because Sir Toby actually hints at a seasonal festivity in his song "O'the twelfth day of December" (II. iii. 84).[3] The opening and closing sections of the scene are worth pausing over. Sir Andrew would clearly be happy to go to bed, but Sir Toby insists on keeping the party going. He is the moving spirit in what is not simply a revel, but rather a revived and maintained revel – against the pressures of those who feel that enough is enough. The scene moves up from the lyric nostalgia of "O Mistress mine" to the bar-room catch, "Hold thy peace", and so to the intense climax of the confrontation: it is then stepped down to the lesser excitements of the projected plot, and finally reverts to the mood of the *piano* opening. Bottom is hit, apparently, with Sir Andrew's Chekhovian "I was adored once too." A moment's silence, a grunt, then "Let's to bed, knight." The scene has ended now, and with it the party? No. Sir Toby, needing more money from Sir Andrew, presses him to send for it; then he changes his mind about going to bed. "Come, come, I'll go burn some sack, 'tis too late to go to bed now. Come, knight, come, knight." And those four monosyllables, which seem to symbolize the energy needed to lug a sack of potatoes from a room, close the scene. Who is there who has not shared and understood this episode? Whatever one's temperament, there is a time to move off and to bed. Someone else prefers to stay and keep things going, though the fire has died out of the occasion. It is a fault of taste, and someone always commits it.

I put it, then, that Sir Toby's interpretation of the Twelfth Night spirit prepares us for, as it is analogous to, his pursuit of the gulling action. Both impulses spring from the same mind. And this leads us to a concept which we have, I think, to contemplate in this play: the likeableness of the dramatis personae.

II

Likeableness, for obvious reasons, is not a critical concept. It looks like an invitation to the untrammelled subjectivities of all readers and playgoers – an abdication of critical decorum. All the same, we need the concept here. That is because Shakespeare, as I view it, sets up a design in which we are to begin by liking certain characters and disliking others, and to end with reversing those judgements.

It is all focused on Sir Toby and Malvolio, though other characters can affect matters marginally. First, let us place Sir Toby, without preconception. I think C. L. Barber's "gentlemanly liberty incarnate"[4] hopelessly over-romanticized, just as I would think "parasite" a misleading importation of modern values concerning employment. It is better to take Sir Toby as a dramatized case-history, with the implied caption "This is the sort of person certain social conditions yield." Sir Toby is a knight; he has no substance, no land or money; he lives with and upon his wealthy kinswoman. The order of relationship was familiar and sanctioned. Having no employment, he is endemically short of things to do, and his activities emerge as drinking, the pursuit of practical jokes, spectator sports, conversation. What else could be expected? Sir Toby is gripped by that ennui which is the condition of the unemployed, at all social levels. More, to base any dramatic system of festive values on Sir Toby is self-evidently absurd, for "holiday" is a meaningless concept save to those who work. Sir Toby does not work, and therefore usurps the values of "play".

His revealed characteristics become steadily less appealing. His drunkenness is nicely poised: in Act II, scene iii it can appear as a tribute to the good life, but in Act I, scene v his brief appearance is all but incoherent. (Perhaps the most telling comment is Olivia's

"By mine honour, *half* drunk" (l. 113). What was the finished product like?) Stage drunkenness is always an ambivalent affair, for the sufficient reason that it is in real life. A drunk is funny, an alcoholic is not. The mind contains diverse views of the matter, and its responses are generally mixed. So in *Twelfth Night*. On the whole, our experience of Sir Toby is in this respect analogous to our reception of anyone who, like the immortal Captain Grimes, "puts in some very plucky work with the elbow": we warm to him more in the earlier than in the later stages of the acquaintance.

Sir Toby's other characteristics are similarly disenchanting. His relationship with Sir Andrew emerges as contemptuous and exploitative. The comic glow protects his name for a while, certainly. Ask anyone who said "Thou hadst need send for more money", and he will likely answer "Iago", and he will be wrong. It is in the gulling actions that Sir Toby appears at his least appealing. There are two main points. He pursues the Malvolio affair with a relentlessness that is disturbing: "I would we were well rid of this knavery. If he may be conveniently deliver'd, I would he were, for I am now so far in offence with my niece that I cannot pursue with any safety this sport to the upshot" (IV. ii. 67–71). Not remorse, but fear of the consequences for himself, inhibits "gentlemanly liberty incarnate" here. No wonder this unattractive little speech is so often cut in performance. The other matter is the gulling of Sir Andrew and the arranged duel between him and Cesario. Here I stress the force of pattern, so often Shakespeare's way of imparting personality and being. One joke is inconclusive. Two suggests a mind obsessively addicted to making sport out of others. It comes back to the ennui of the unemployed, and therefore to the social attitudes that condition Sir Toby's cast of mind.

III

"Art any more than a steward?" Everyone quotes the great tribute to cakes and ale; fewer recall, or perhaps in the audience even register, the words that immediately precede it. The greater quotation drives out the lesser. It is typical of this play's strategy that the reservation is set into the record, before being overtaken by the main tenor of the play's surface statement. Yet the question summarizes much of the play's concerns and tensions. All Shakespeare's plays exhibit some social tensions, if only within the same class. *Twelfth Night*, more than any other comedy of this period, reveals a discreet awareness of these tensions. Three of its personages marry upwards (Sebastian, Viola, Maria) and two seek to (Sir Andrew, Malvolio). This movement upwards is caricatured in Malvolio, but the others demonstrate it too. There is a general blurring of social frontiers in Olivia's household, and this contributes to the friction and resentments of the play. Malvolio is the administrator, formally in charge, and he has to deal with people who are or feel themselves to be socially superior to him. It recalls the resentments that Drake identified years before: "I must have the gentleman to haul and draw with the mariner, and the mariners with the gentleman." These resentments, dramatized most forcefully in the encounters of Malvolio and Sir Toby, are in fact most subtly expressed through Maria.

Maria need not be seen and played as the bouncy, vital soubrette of stage history.[5] Her pattern is one of social resentment, a willingness to stir up trouble for others (while usually exiting rapidly from the scene of the crime), and a remorseless drive towards her post-curtain apotheosis: Lady Belch. (Her route there is charted via the subtextually unimpeachable "do not think I have wit enough to lie straight in my bed", and whatever the director wants to make of "Come by and by to my chamber"). With Maria, conversations tend to turn into threats to others. Sir Toby is in trouble; Feste may be fired; Cesario should be shown the door; Malvolio will come; Malvolio is mad. Maria's "perfectly selfless tact"[6] is invisible to me. As with Sir Toby, we must reach out for a type from the characteristics of the individual. Maria endures the classic ambivalences of the lady-in-waiting, above the servants but not ranking with the great. Who is Maria? "My niece's chambermaid" is Sir Toby's description, in her presence. It is not what we should term an introduction: Sir Toby is speaking to Sir Andrew, presumably just out of earshot of Maria. The editorial glosses are unanimous in their assurance that "My niece's chambermaid" means "lady-in-waiting" or "lady's maid". But the *OED* does not confirm that certitude. The fact is that *chambermaid* did also, at this time, mean (as we should expect) "female servant", roughly the usage of today. Interestingly, the *OED* marks the "lady's maid" sense of *chambermaid* as obsolete: the latest reference cited is Swift's, in 1719. In other words, the editors limit the word to a sense destined to become historically moribund (perhaps, already so), while rejecting a perfectly healthy sense that has survived to our present day. I don't, of course, doubt that the editorial gloss substantially identifies the position Maria holds in Olivia's household. (Olivia herself refers to Maria as "my gentlewoman", I. v. 160.) I suggest that the "servant" sense is present, and in Maria's mind; which is why Sir Toby does not speak the word to Maria's face. *Chambermaid* indicates a historic trap, out of which the most socially agile clambered – upwards. Why they should wish to is touched in during Act I, scene v. Maria receives a deadly thrust from Cesario: her nautically phrased intervention is met with "No, good *swabber*, I am to hull here a little longer" (ll. 199–200), after which no more is heard from Maria. *Swabber* is one who swabs down decks – and is therefore pure metaphor – but contains the lingering hint that Maria was engaged in a similar activity, as *chambermaid*. The social insult is part of what the play identifies as the fluid and shifting lines of social demarcation.[7]

IV

In the collisions of aspiration and resentment Malvolio stands, or seems to stand, for an absurd and affected species of folly. That is the unmistakable verdict that we are required to arrive at in the first half of *Twelfth Night*. Yet the play's strategy is to pivot the dramatis personae around on their revolving stage, and the second half is insistent that we reconsider Malvolio. Notoriously, this poses problems for the actor. It is fairly easy to play the Malvolio of the first few scenes; it is fairly easy to play the Malvolio of the later scenes; it is difficult to knit the two halves into a whole, which is one reason why Malvolio is a star part. There are difficulties for the audience, and for the critic, too, since all are engaged in revising a settled position. As we look back on the early scenes, a few obvious points can be ticked off. Malvolio is a charmless and humourless bureaucrat, but honest and able, and Olivia thinks well of him. ("I would not have him miscarry for the half of my dowry", III. iv. 64–5.) It cannot be easy to get Sir Toby to behave – Olivia cannot – and the functional opposition between them slips easily into antagonism. Then, the drinking scene (II. iii) is presented entirely from the view of the partygoers. We, the audience, are at the party, and we want it to go on. Yet everyone has had the experience of being woken up in the small hours by a crowd of late revellers, and of feeling precisely the rage that Malvolio puts words to (acting on behalf of Olivia, and Malvolio would never lie on a matter like that). That rage is the greater if one needs to get up to *work* – unlike the revellers, who can sleep it off. In the theatre there is only one case, that of the partygoers. In real life there is a quite different case, and our backward glance recognizes it. Malvolio, then, is not the simple anti-life stereotype he is cast for in Act ii, scene iii. But the on-stage case for Malvolio does not emerge until Act iv, scene ii.

The cell scene is crucial. On the one side, we begin to detach ourselves from the sustained animosity of Feste, and from the self-interested sadism of Sir Toby. On the other, we recognize a "different" human being, emerging from the darkness. It is a rebirth, almost. I do not wish to support some of the excesses of stage history. Henry Irving, for instance, used to play the scene all out for pathos, with much weeping and an appeal to the "poor man" response.[8] What happens to Malvolio has nothing to do with pathos. It is a matter of human identity emerging, and it is all in the words. Take, as a simple comparison, Malvolio's opening lines, "Yes, and shall do, till the pangs of death shake him. Infirmity, that decays the wise, doth ever make the better fool . . . I marvel your ladyship takes delight in such a barren rascal" (i. v. 72–81). It is impossible to speak these lines without giving in some form the impression of an affected dolt. And now take:

> I say this house is as dark as ignorance, though ignorance were as dark as hell; and I say there was never man thus abus'd. I am no more mad than you are; make the trial of it in any constant question. . . . I think nobly of the soul, and no way approve his opinion.   (iv. ii. 46–56)

Unless one strains intolerably against the direction of the words, it is impossible to speak them in the manner and accent of a fool. They express a being of sense, and human worth. The words must be respected, and thus the speaker. Above all, the words express an identity, individual and social.

And what is this identity? It is that of a gentleman. The first phase of the cell scene, the dialogue with Sir Topas, shows Malvolio at bottom. This is the dark night of the soul, the communion with madness and (apparently) clerical imbecility. The second phase, with Feste speaking in his own voice, records Malvolio's struggle out of the pit and towards the light. The themes are communication, relationship, ways and means. Phase two starts with the calls of "Fool!" (which Feste affects not to hear) and, after "Who calls, ha?", modulates into "*Good* fool". What follows is decisive:

> Good fool, as ever thou wilt deserve well at my hand, help me to a candle, and pen, ink, and paper. As I am a gentleman, I will live to be thankful to thee for't.   (ll. 80–3)

The identity which Malvolio discovers for himself in the cell, and which he imparts to us, is the backing for his promise: "As I am a gentleman." Not, be it noted, "steward". The identity of functional authority is rejected in favour of a term whose core of meaning lies outside, as well as within, social rank. The *OED* does not commit itself to a categorization of Malvolio's word here – neither does Schmidt nor Onions – but I judge sense 3 to be the nearest: "A man in whom gentle birth is accompanied by appropriate qualities of behaviour; hence, in general, a man of chivalrous instincts and fine feelings." *Gentleman*, of all social terms, casts the widest net. The word contains the ideas of birth, education, wealth, behaviour and values; yet it allows no single aspect to dominate, nor can any element insist on its presence. *Gentleman*, that uniquely English invention, is at bottom the principle of "tolerance" within the social structure, the moving part that takes the strain of fixed relationships.[9] It is also, in dramatic terms, a variable, and it permits a case to be reopened and the standing of Malvolio to be reconsidered, very late.[10] The term accounts for Malvolio's changed address to the Fool. Malvolio does not offer him a crude bribe, but a form of words that combines the hint of material reward with the understatements of courtesy. "I will live to be thankful to thee for't. . . . It shall advantage thee more than ever the bearing of letter did. . . . Fool, I'll requite it to the highest degree" (IV. ii. 82–3, 111–12, 118). Under all is the implied admission of fellowship with the Fool. Not "fellow", that socially ambivalent word Malvolio mistook from Olivia, but fellowship, is Malvolio's discovery. The man who would be "Count Malvolio", fantasy's alternative to "Steward", now founds himself on the truth of "gentleman".

Shakespeare admits the claim, for Malvolio at the end speaks the language of a gentleman. Before his final irruption occurs the inter-mezzo of the letter. This episode throws some light on the dramatic origins of Fabian. Commentators have often wondered as to the point of this nondescript character, who appears, as few characters in Shakespeare do, to have been less created than manufactured.[11]

Of the functional reasons for his existence, the most important that I can detect is his reading of Malvolio's letter. We need Fabian for the same reason that we need a newscaster for news: we require a fairly neutral and objective tone for the delivery of potentially explosive information. By universal assent, a too emotional, personal delivery distracts one's reception of the message. Feste's hatred of Malvolio bars a neutral reading, and he obviously mimics Malvolio's voice; hence Olivia orders Fabian to read the letter. His colourless delivery is exactly the right medium, and the message comes through with undisturbed clarity. Malvolio's deep sense of injury is expressed with both passion and control, and the Duke's comment ratifies its inner decorum: "This savours not much of distraction." (This line is a perfectly formed cell in the structure of the final scene: the aesthete's word, "savour", confronts a reality outside the world of aesthetic contemplation.) Malvolio's is a well-filed message, and by dramatic convention it is, like almost all letters, expressed in prose.

Hence the way is paved for Malvolio's entry, and his climactic statement of injury. The tone and quality of that last speech are obvious to all. What matters formally is that the speech is in verse. For the first time in the play, Malvolio speaks in the language of the rank to which he had aspired. It is his ultimate irony, that in the moment of humiliation and disgrace he speaks in the tongue of social elevation and human dignity.

V

That final speech, leading to the appalling "I'll be reveng'd on the whole pack of you", is the climax of everything that happens in *Twelfth Night*. That experience must be confronted, and neither denied nor indulged. "Malvolio: a Tragedy" is a sentimentalization of this play. But equally, one is struck by the large number of critics who, on this issue, seem bent on repressing instincts which, outside the theatre of *Twelfth Night*, they would surely admit. I cite a few instances, though my point could easily be illustrated at far greater length. To Joseph Summers, "Malvolio is, of course, justly punished."[12] Barbara K. Lewalski concurs in the natural justice of the affair: "Since he so richly deserves his exposure, and so actively cooperates in bringing it upon himself, there seems little warrant for the critical tears sometimes shed over his harsh

treatment and none at all for a semi-tragic rendering of his plight in
the 'dark house'."[13] For C. L. Barber, Malvolio is "a kind of foreign
body to be expelled by laughter, in Shakespeare's last free-and-easy
festive comedy".[14] Most certainly he is to be expelled, if *Twelfth
Night* is a "free-and-easy festive comedy"; but supposing the in-
truder belongs in the play, what then?

How can one explain this critical imperviousness to the ending?
One comes to view the critics here as a representative sampling of
the human mind. They *want*, as we all do, a comedy; they do not
want a disturbance to the agreeable mood created in *Twelfth Night*;
it is easiest to find a response based on "Serve Malvolio right: he
asked for it: anyway, Olivia and Orsino will do their best to
smoothe things over." They seek a formula that helps to suppress
the disquiet one inevitably feels. In this they faithfully embody
certain tendencies within the mind, and thus – as Shakespeare well
knew – of this audience.

Even so, it is a failure of criticism. Hardin Craig catches the
essence of the position I have illustrated, commenting that the
reading of Malvolio's last line "is by many modern actors so
passionate and revengeful as to spoil the effect of the comedy; this
cannot have been Shakespeare's intention".[15] Precisely: but it is
only necessary to extend the thought an inch further, and ask: was it
not Shakespeare's intention to "spoil the effect of the comedy", and
was not that the goal to which the entire dramatic enterprise was
directed? Why not? Where is it laid down that a dramatist may not
build into his design a threat to its own mood?

In the final stages, that threat all but destroys the mood of *Twelfth
Night*. The minor action bids to overwhelm the major. The Illyrian
world of fulfilled romance, genial comics and harmless pranks
metamorphoses into an image of the real world, with its grainy
texture, social frictions, and real pain inflicted upon real people.
Malvolio must bear the burden of the real world, as he did its festive
release. The disposable person of part one has become the victim of
part two, and thus the agent for showing up the festive spirit itself.
The Duke's last nine lines exactly measure the play's attempt to
pull together the vestiges of the mood of comedy. But this time the
party, barring a last song from Feste, is really over. It is balm of a
sort, and the audience needs it, for it has to recover from a climax in
which it participated, to the origins of which it was privy. It is
necessary for the mind's defences to re-group. They have, after all,
to deal with shock.

"*I'll be reveng'd on the whole pack of you.*" The theatrical dimension of the line is all-important, and we need the historical imagination to grasp it. At *pack,* the subliminal metaphor discloses itself. It is a bear-baiting. The audience becomes spectators, Malvolio the bear. The theatrical voltage of the shock is immensely increased if we accept that bear-baiting actually occurred within the same auditorium.[16] It is, however, unnecessary for me to argue here that theatres were "multi-use auditoria". The essential point is that the original audience would have witnessed enough bear-baitings, whether in the specific theatre of *Twelfth Night* (Globe), in other theatres such as the Hope, or elsewhere. The connections between theatre, bear-baiting and festivity were well established.[17] And the awareness of those connections would have governed the audience's experience of Malvolio. So would the delivery of the line. We see a Malvolio who must address his stage tormentors, roughly at right angles to the sight lines of the audience. He is addressing Orsino and company, not us. Imagine a Malvolio in the centre of the platform stage,[18] addressing others downstage: he is surrounded on three (or all) sides by tiers of spectators, who are still perhaps jeering at him, and turns on his heel through at least 180 degrees to take in "the whole *pack of you*". That way the house, not merely the stage company, is identified with the "pack". It is theatre as blood sport, theatre that celebrates its own dark origins. That, too, is "festive" comedy. What the audience makes of its emotions is its own affair. I surmise that the ultimate effect of *Twelfth Night* is to make the audience ashamed of itself.

6 Communal Identity and the Rituals of *Julius Caesar*

"Toute ma vie, je me suis fait une certaine idée de la France", wrote de Gaulle in the introduction to his memoirs. A certain idea of Rome dominates *Julius Caesar*, ordering and explaining the play. Without this idea of Rome, the accounts of *Julius Caesar* will be lacking in vital tissue. The approach via character ("But Cassius is a realist"[1]) was evidently exhausted long ago. To see the political issues in contemporary terms – Caesar a dictator, Brutus an ineffective liberal – is appealing, but ultimately unconvincing. Politics are rooted in the specifics of community, and much of *Julius Caesar* is untranslatable. Nor can the obvious political categories be taken for granted: Beerbohm Tree used to present Caesar as a liberal Shavian reformer, not a tyrant.[2] Anthropology, then? The aftermath of the assassination connects the play to a powerful ritual, the priestly slaying of a victim. Yet this is a localized, as much as a universal action. And Shakespeare does not invoke what might seem the most inviting of myths, that of Prometheus the Tyrant-challenger.[3] Slaying the Tyrant will not do as a statement of the archetypal action of *Julius Caesar*. Nor will the Killing of Father. Shakespeare makes no use of the tradition that Brutus was Caesar's son – if anything, he preserves the suggestion of a son role for Antony (III. i. 22).[4] The obvious myths do not fit the play. We come back to Rome, as the social determinant of the action.

The omnipresence of Rome needs no demonstration, but the statistics are worth registering. Taking together "Rome", "Roman", "Romans", we find in Act I 19 references; 16 in Act II; 23 in Act III; 4 in Act IV; and 11 in Act V. These figures conform to one's sense of the play's rhythm, that after a strong, assertive opening the climax is reached in Act III, and a slackening of tension in Act IV leads up to the Roman apotheosis. The idea of Rome fades as the action removes itself from Rome, and returns with the Roman

75

suicides and valedictories. Moreover, the idea of Rome has absolute command. This is not one of Shakespeare's dual location schemes, and there are no Egyptians or Volscians to challenge the Roman idea. The battlefield of Philippi is simply a cockpit where Romans settle their differences, not a focus of values external to Rome. The audience is never allowed to forget that *Julius Caesar* is a Roman play.

While the physical presence of Rome makes itself continually felt (throughout the first three acts), the meaning of "Roman" is the play's chief subject. Naturally, the term is analysed in the main through the leading actors. But not entirely: the crowd is the raw energy of Rome, a vessel for the primitive violence in the city which also expresses itself through the Roman leaders. The crowd is, if you like, a kind of collective subconscious, a physical realization of a layer in the Roman mind." . . . the state of man, / Like to a little kingdom, suffers then / The nature of an insurrection": the revolt of Act III, Scenes ii and iii is the insurrection in Brutus's mind. As Coghill observes of the lynching of Cinna, "It is an epiphany of Rome in forty lines."[5] It is: and that violence directs us back to examine the upper layers of the Roman mind, to explain the explosion of Act III and the outcome of Act V. In this search we shall need to move between the Rome of history and the Rome of Shakespeare, recognizing the authenticity basic to Shakespeare's design: "part of his intention was a serious effort at representing the Roman scene as genuinely as he could".[6]

I

"This Roman morality", says Grimal, "has a very distinct aim – the subordination of the individual to the City."[7] Only in the Roman plays does such a concept inform Shakespeare's drama. Of course Shakespeare always creates a society with its own value-system, but this system, outside the Roman plays, is not focused to an ideology of place. The framework of that civic morality – *virtus, pietas, fides* – can be taken for granted here. What concerns us is the mechanism through which Rome grips the individual. The City rules; and its moral instrument is patriarchy.

That Shakespeare had grasped this appears in the opening lines of *Titus Andronicus:*

Saturninus   Noble patricians, patrons of my right,
Defend the justice of my cause with arms;
And, countrymen, my loving followers,
Plead my successive title with your swords.
I am his first-born son, that was the last
That wore the imperial diadem of Rome.
Then let my father's honours live in me,
Nor wrong mine age with this indignity.

(I. i. 1–8)

Bassianus, the younger brother, pleads for "desert in pure election", but Titus decides in favour of "our Emperor's eldest son, / Lord Saturninus" (228–9). It is a clear announcement of the idea governing the dramatic development. The play then becomes an extended analysis of the system's distortions, stemming from a rigid and unfeeling code of patriarchy. *Titus Andronicus* clears the way for the vastly subtler analysis of patriarchy in *Julius Caesar*. The point about fathers in *Titus Andronicus* is that they have children, over whom they exercise total authority. The point about the dramatis personae in *Julius Caesar* is that they have fathers, but no children. Caesar speaks of the "sterile curse" of Calpurnia; no one else has or speaks of children. (Antony has a nephew, IV. i. 5.[8]) Caesar is at least aware of a problem, one might say. No one else is. And all the dramatic energies of the patriarchal system, since children are (dramatically) excluded, are directed in upon the self as a reflection of ancestry.

The shift from patriarchy (basically, as it affects fathers) in *Titus Andronicus,* to patriarchy as it affects children in *Julius Caesar,* is profound and all-pervasive. I read it as in essence a development of thought which owes its origins to the interior logic of the canon: the society of *Julius Caesar* succeeds the society of *Titus Andronicus*. Now in the chronology of history the order is reversed; and Trevor Nunn, who directed the four Roman plays as a tetralogy (RSC, 1972), choose to end with *Titus Andronicus*. He argued that *Titus Andronicus* is a study in the decadence of Rome. One sees the point. I prefer, however, to accept the canonical order as the imprint of thought, and thus of the historical imagination in Shakespeare. In other words, I view the society of *Titus Andronicus* not as decadent, but as primitive; the true decadence emerges in *Julius Caesar*.

Of what, then, does this decadence consist? It shows itself through the intense sense of ancestry that the Romans display. It verges on ancestor worship. "I am the son of Marcus Cato, ho!" cries young Cato (v. iv. 4, 6). "Think you I am no stronger than my sex, / Being so father'd and so husbanded?" asks Portia (ii. i. 296–7). "But woe the while, our fathers' minds are dead" says Cassius (i. iii. 82). *Father* in *Julius Caesar* is not an immediate progenitor, a person one actually knows. Father is subsumed into *patres*, City fathers, elders; he is an ancestor, a standard of conduct, an ideal. "I, as Aeneas, our great ancestor" says Cassius (i. ii. 112). "My ancestors did from the streets of Rome / The Tarquin drive, when he was called a king" says Brutus (ii. i. 43–4). The highest praise that Caius Ligarius can bestow on Brutus, "Soul of Rome! Brave son, deriv'd from honourable loins!" fuses ancestry with the life of the City (ii. i. 321–2). Even over several generations, the patriarchal grip is fastened upon the minds of Romans.

The obsessive awareness of ancestry crystallizes into the importance attached to statuary. In a superficial enough sense, the statue is the characteristic expressive form of Rome. It is hard, marble, an unrelenting assertion of self that one has to accept or overturn. In a deeper sense, the statue expresses the continuing spiritual life of the family and the City. There existed

> the custom, indeed the right, by which noble families set up in a recess of the central hall of their houses, at first, wax-masks and, later, busts of their ancestors who had deserved well of their family or of the state.[9]

Thus a statue (or image, or mask) had a significance for a Roman totally missing from, say, that of a Victorian statesman for his public. *Julius Caesar* catches if it does not expound this significance. Flavius and Marullus know that to have the Caesarian images disrobed is a vital symbolic challenge, just as Caesar knows that it must be met by having them "put to silence". The grotesque comparison between Caesar and the Colossus is chosen to inflame Brutus further. Cassius instructs Cinna to set up one of the anonymous letters to Brutus "Upon old Brutus' statue". Calpurnia's dream, as related by Caesar, realizes him as a statue running blood. Caesar dies at the foot of Pompey's statue, not a shallow irony of personality but an antithesis of stage expression: the statue and the man, the marble and the flesh. The statue as a metaphor for identity, that is the play's proposal; and the Roman crowd, in its own way, assents. "Give him a statue with his ancestors" (iii. ii. 50) is their tribute to Brutus (coupled with the naively ironic "Let him be Caesar").

Statue is a public rendering of name. Patriarchy must code itself into a system of names, and the Romans are excessively conscious of nomenclature. They refer often to their names as a kind of externalized self. This trick of third-person reference, which everyone notices, can be easily misjudged. Commentators detect it most easily in Caesar himself, and are apt to see the trait as evidence of Caesar's "arrogance".[10] How can this be so, if others exhibit the same trait? "Cassius from bondage will deliver Cassius" (I. iii. 90); "You speak to Casca, and to such a man" (I. iii. 116); "When Marcus Brutus grows so covetous" (IV. iii. 79). They all do it. Caesar is in this one who focuses and magnifies traits in the Roman mind. I cannot, therefore, follow John Velz's reading that "The dominance of Caesarism is also suggested by the fact that numerous other characters . . . adopt Caesar's characteristic trick of speech."[11] An element of imitation can fairly be accepted here. But to regard the whole characteristic as a bad speech habit which the Romans picked up from listening to Caesar is surely to miss an ingrained Roman mode of thought and expression. The name acts as a model of self, imparting a standard of conduct to which Romans are to adhere.

II

So far, our alignment runs: Rome; patriarchy; statue; name. The alignment holds into what is clearly the key concept, role. It has received some critical attention since Anne Righter's seminal *Shakespeare and the Idea of the Play*. Van Laan analyses the action of *Julius Caesar* in terms of ironically discrepant role-playing; for him, each of the actors takes on a role he cannot fulfil. *Julius Caesar* is a play of ironic o'erparting.[12] Similarly, Velz concentrates on the way in which characters adopt roles which other characters have played. "Role-playing is, then, crucial to the plot of *Julius Caesar* . . . The republicans see themselves in roles from the heroic past, while the monarchists look to a prototype who appears onstage and who belongs fully to the Rome of the present."[13] I should place a different emphasis on the matter. The Romans are playing the roles, not of others, but of themselves. Identity, and not imitation, is the goal towards which Roman behaviour is directed.

The name is the role. The patronymic encodes the data of ancestry and behaviour which a Roman should embody.[14] Let Cassius focus the argument:

> Brutus and Caesar. What should be in that "Caesar"?
> Why should that name be sounded more than yours?
> Write them together, yours is as fair a name;
> Sound them, it doth become the mouth as well;
> Weigh them, it is as heavy; conjure with 'em,
> "Brutus" will start a spirit as soon as "Caesar".
>
> (I. ii. 142–7)

Only, I think, in *Romeo and Juliet* (III. iii) is there elsewhere in the canon such a sense of name as containing vital essence, of name as an objective reality in itself. Cassius's speech here contains the main idea of what Rome is (a Republic), and what, therefore, a Roman should be. But the psychological objective of all Romans is to discover themselves through the affirmation of name and *Roman*. "Was that done like Cassius?" asks Brutus (IV. iii. 77). "Then like a Roman bear the truth I tell" Messala enjoins Brutus (IV. iii. 187). "He will be found like Brutus, like himself" Lucilius assures Antony (V. iv. 25). To find oneself is ideologically simple, whatever the stresses involved. One refers problems to the role to solve.

Role as motive is the explanation of the provocative "It must be by his death", which vaults over all argument to assert a prior conclusion. Schanzer remarks that

> It would seem that Shakespeare wishes us to feel that the decision had nothing to do with reason and logic, that he has somehow fallen victim to Cassius' rhetoric without being able to accept his arguments or share his motives. What we are watching in this soliloquy is Brutus' attempt to defend his decision before the court of his conscience.[15]

It is the decision, and not the defence, that concerns us here. The decision is a hardening of primary structures of mind and being, an acquiescence in the most basic imperatives of name and role. The entire movement of the opening conducts Brutus to the realization that he has no choice. After the acquiescence in role, the role governs all decisions.

The role, of course, slips often; and this fact is one of the main roads into the interior play. We can get at it in several ways. *Julius Caesar,* for all its emphasis on hard men with hard values, shows continually another side. "The whole is suffused with a soft emotionalism." "No other play of Shakespeare concentrates more on 'emotion', 'heart', 'love'."[16] These Romans constantly assert an identity that leaves unassuaged large areas of their minds. The heroic figure of the Roman imagination stands often beyond the fumblings of the play's personages, and one can find in this "echoes of absurdity".[17] Without labouring the available ironies, we ought to take in the ways in which the Romans assume, let slip, and reimpose their versions of themselves. It is all focused on the most representative Roman figure: Julius Caesar.

The apparently simple opening words of Caesar throw an immediate challenge to the interpreter of motives:

> *Caesar*   Calpurnia! . . .
> Stand you directly in Antonius' way,
> When he doth run his course. Antonius! . . .
> Forget not, in your speed, Antonius,
> To touch Calpurnia; for our elders say,
> The barren, touched in this holy chase,
> Shake off their sterile curse.
> (I. ii. 1–9)

A bystander might react variously:

1. Caesar wants a child, a family.
2. He wants to please his wife.
3. He wants to found a dynasty.
4. As a good politician, he participates in a long-established custom, much beloved of the people.

Other motives are easily discoverable, but these suffice. The human and political tensions, so evident, elsewhere, are at once presented. And now Antony says something rather interesting: "I shall remember. / When Caesar says 'do this', it is performed." One can read this as part of the atmosphere of an "oriental court".[18] To me, Antony is *reminding* Caesar of his role. Caesar cannot be rebuked; but it is possible for the Roman establishment, through Antony, to say in effect "Rest assured, Caesar, that your lightest word is a

solemn command: we know our function too."[19] Later, "I rather
tell thee what is to be fear'd, / Than what I fear; for always I am
Caesar" (I. ii. 211–12). The role slips, and is (rather apologetically)
self-adjusted. Caesar is sensitive to Antony's earlier "Fear him
not, Caesar", since Romans do not fear. The same struggle occurs
in II. ii, when Caesar finds it vitally important to assert his role. The
phrasing is suggestive in

> And tell them that I will not come today.
> Cannot, is false, and that I dare not, falser;
> I will not come today.
>
> (II. ii. 62–4)

It is as though Caesar makes a subliminal slip, which he openly
corrects.

Decius acts in full co-operation with Caesar. He appears less a
flatterer than a kind of courtly *chef de protocole,* deeply concerned
about his own role and the Senate's reception of Caesar's absence.
"Most mighty / Caesar, let me know some cause, / Lest I be laugh'd
at when I tell them so" (ll. 69–70). Equally, we can see him as a
member of Buckingham's tribe, versed in public relations and
solicitous of his client's image in the world. Decius's response is
"This will never do, Caesar" and it is irresistible. The Roman
establishment is its own most effective reminder of conduct.

In Caesar can be observed the quintessence of Roman-ness.
Roman behaviour is directed always towards answering the question: what would Caesar (or Brutus, Cassius, etc.) do in my
position? Caesar, answering for all, says: Caesar would behave
Caesarianly. And he does so. Only the role slips, and he has to
adjust it, rather self-consciously. In this he receives the sympathetic
co-operation of other Romans. The role of Caesar is undoubtedly
approved socially, notwithstanding that the role collides with the
Republican tradition. It is clear that Caesar, in asserting the
precedent of the *dictator* (Sulla, for example) and receiving the
sycophantic support of the Senate, does in fact embody a Roman
tradition. The opposed traditions combine through the hard mask
of public manners, and Caesar displays this too in

> Good friends, go in, and taste some wine with me,
> And we, like friends, will straightway go together.
>
> (II. ii. 127–8)

Caesar cannot have failed to gauge the underlying hostilities. His "like friends" is most suggestive: it imparts that Romans, even when politically opposed, possess a model of public behaviour that enables them to compose their differences.[20] In this as in all else, Caesar plays out a publicly sanctioned role.

III

We can now read the assassination, the moment that expresses most intensely everything that is Roman in *Julius Caesar*. Once Caesar has decided to don his robe (a public garment[21]) and go to the Capitol, he enters upon a final phase in the dramatic programming, in which all steps are inevitable and irreversible. "The ides of March are come": Caesar cannot ignore the Soothsayer, has to state his own sense of challenge and survival. Since Caesar addresses the Soothsayer, Artemidorus has his cue to join in and bid Caesar "Read this schedule." Decius (presumably sensing the danger) immediately presses Trebonius' suit, which incites Artemidorus to the fatal "O Caesar, read mine first, for mine's a suit / That touches Caesar nearer." Caesar has no choice now. His role requires him to respond "What touches us ourself shall be last serv'd." The illusion of individual freedom yields to the exigencies of the programming. There follows the Popilian interlude, of which it need only be observed that the possibility of intervention and failure comes from outside; the conspirators keep their nerve. (Compare the quarrelling and unsupportive conspirators in *Henry IV*.) With the conspirators, as with Caesar, roles are enforced from the beginning of Act III, scene i. Just as the importunities of Artemidorus make Caesar Caesar, so the Popilian threat and the presence of each other conduce to ultra-Roman behaviour.

This is a public occasion; and the Romans, with their natural bent for display, rise to the utmost of their public selves. There is a communal pattern of intensification and exaggeration. It is already governed by the movements of a ritual. Metellus overplays the suppliant, and this in turn elicits Caesar's overstatements of his own role.

> I must prevent thee, Cimber.
> These couchings and these lowly courtesies
> Might fire the blood of ordinary men,

> And turn preordinance and first decree
> Into the law of children.
>
> (III. i. 35–9)

"Preordinance and first decree", usually glossed on the lines of "what has been ordained and decreed from the first",[22] has surely a hint of challenge to primogeniture, and thus to patriarchy. Metellus is now joined by Brutus and Cassius, each kneeling; so Caesar is ringed with suppliants. Caesar has passed beyond the functional grandeur of "What is now amiss / That Caesar and his Senate must redress?" (III. i. 31–2) and now embarks on the magniloquence of the "northern star" speech, which indeed makes the impression of a tyrant far gone in megalomania. But one can as well argue that it is stimulated by the posturing of Metellus and the others, and this in turn arises from the induction "Are we all ready?", itself a cue to the conspirators. In the mutuality of behaviour and response, which stimulus comes first? As I read the scene, history is reduced to choreography. Each actor is cast for a role in which he is compelled to play out an epic drama of Roman history, a myth of the City: the *dictator*-King is slain by the keepers of the Republican tradition. And yet, such is the rivalry within the Roman tradition, the word that triggers off the ultimate response is a word the conspirators have already chosen for their own ("Cassius, be constant"): Caesar's final speech is a paean upon the theme of "constant",[23] a word thrice struck, and the speech concludes upon the intolerable challenge of

> Let me a little show it even in this –
> That I was constant Cimber should be banish'd,
> And constant do remain to keep him so.
>
> (70–2)

It is the same insight Shakespeare preserved for the opening of *King Lear* ("By Jupiter, / This shall not be revok'd"): there are times when the Prince must hold his ground, regardless of the consequences. So with those who confront him. And so the convulsive movements of the ritual take charge over the words and actions of the Romans. At the moment of the slaying, there are no individuals, only roles.

The ritual idea surfaces for inspection in "Stoop, Romans, stoop / And let us bathe our hands in Caesar's blood" (105–6). This is open, and can be looked at variously. Brents Stirling has shown how formal allusions to ritual and ceremony order *Julius Caesar,* and how the assassination is a "conversion of bloodshed to ritual".[24] Psychologically, Brutus's injunction makes good sense as high-minded self-exculpation, a desire to avoid the personal guilt of killing; the conspirators de-personalize the event by relating it to a ritual. And indeed, Brutus is anxious to merge the assassination into Roman usage, "Caesar shall / Have all true rites and lawful ceremonies" (III. i. 241–2). After all, an execution was to the Romans an act of consecration to the gods; the term *sacer esto* was the Roman death sentence. I would stress that the "ritual" manifestation is a revelation of what the inner forces are: a drive towards the realization of self as an actor in a ritual. When Brutus urges the conspirators to "bear it as our Roman actors do" (II. i. 226) he touches a deep vein of civic conduct and identity. The actors of the future whom Cassius invokes ("How many ages hences / Shall this our lofty scene be acted over") match the actors of the present. For "actor", like other terms in this play, is not really a universal counter. It denotes a model of behaviour that is profoundly Roman. Actors, like statues, exist to remind the Romans of themselves.

IV

The roles which sustain the conspirators through the crisis lose much of their vitality and meaning in Acts IV and V. Brutus and Cassius become weary automata, playing out their parts with a diminishing expectation of success. Their roles fail to master the situations of quarrel and civil conflict; and because they are felt to be inadequate, they are asserted the more vehemently. The "enforced ceremony" (IV. ii. 21) marks the cooling of Cassius's regard for Brutus. Brutus has to remind Cassius of the past, "Remember March, the ides of March remember" (IV. ii. 18). And the "Roman actor" ideal is the unacknowledged premise of conduct for Brutus in the quarrel scene. The replay of Portia's death I read not as a textual problem of alternative versions, but as a straightforward statement of exaggeration.[25] Brutus needs to play out before his subordinates the role of Stoic Roman, a transaction solemnized by

Brutus Now, as you are a Roman, tell me true.
Messala Then like a Roman bear the truth I tell.
(186–7)

The role takes the strain of the personal anguish, expressed in the private encounter with Cassius. I do not think there are real difficulties here: Brutus takes the role to the point of caricature. So, for that matter, does Portia.

There is, in fact, only one function which the Roman role can govern successfully in the later stages: it is the mastering of defeat. The enterprise of the conspirators is evidently doomed; Caesar's ghost is the spirit, "hot from hell", that has joined the *manes* to be appeased. Even ancestry, then, turns against the conspirators. What is left is purely resolution. Cassius is "resolv'd / To meet all perils very *constantly*" (v. i. 90–1). Since the ultimate degradation is to be "led in triumph / Through the streets of Rome" (v. i. 108–9), Brutus strikes a pose of third-person heroics that is quite as mannered as Caesar's last words:

> Think not, thou noble Roman,
> That ever Brutus will go bound to Rome:
> He bears too great a mind.
>
> (v. i. 110–12)

If Caesar had said that, the commentators would still be reproving him for measureless arrogance, for exhibiting all the linguistic stigmata of a tyrant. As will be clear by now, I think such a judgement misconceived. That is simply the way the Romans are.

The suicides are the only true Roman acts left to the conspirators. In committing them, they receive the approval and tributes of their fellow Romans. That approval is extended to Strato, as loyal servant and instrument of Brutus's suicide; his services are rewarded with employment under Octavius. There remain the valedictories of Antony and Octavius. Of them, let us register the minor but not unimportant irony that Brutus, in this play of names, is not mentioned by name. He receives what posthumous rehabilitation is possible, by being accorded the tribute of "this was the noblest Roman of them all". Antony's voice is choric, and thus the community's. In death as in life Brutus is permitted to manifest the characteristics of the tribe. Rome will always find its formulas for the survival of the State. It is the correct reduction of a play founded on the subordination of the individual part to the whole.

I propose, then, that the roots of the tragic action in *Julius Caesar* lie in communal identity; and that the actors, in asserting their individuality, do so by responding to impulses that emanate from the collective mind. The ambivalence of "act", so exhaustively explored in the canon, is here defined in terms of Roman society. What the Romans imitate is their ancestry; what they aspire to be is the reflection of the dead. Always their names stand to them as a gauge of conduct, a living tribunal over which their ancestors preside. Hence the play becomes, in a very Roman way, a sacrifice to one's ancestors. It is perhaps the most pessimistic, the most unillusioned of all Shakespearean tragedies, this vision of a society that knows no other way of defining its present, no other exit from its past. In the end even the individuality of the name disappears, lost in the collective formation. Like *Hamlet*, this play poses the question, "Who's there?" (i. ii. 41). Unlike *Hamlet*, it supplies an answer: "A Roman".

7 Masques and Dumb Shows in Webster

In the second Act of *The White Devil*, immediately following Bracciano's conversation with Dr Julio, Monticelso hands Camillo a paper:

> *Monticelso* Here is an emblem nephew – pray peruse it.
>   'Twas thrown in at your window, –
> *Camillo*   At my window?
>   Here is a stag my lord hath shed his horns,
>   And for the loss of them the poor beast weeps –
>   The word "Inopem me copia fecit".
> *Monticelso* That is,
>   Plenty of horns hath made him poor of horns.

Camillo might well change the subject at this point, but obligingly pursues it:

>   What should this mean?
> *Monticelso*   I'll tell you, – 'tis given out
>   You are a cuckold.
>   (II. i. 323–31)

The passage is not conspicuously successful, because of its highly literary quality. We do not see the emblem, the image of the stag, merely a piece of paper whose contents and meaning are described to us. Nevertheless it is a cell in the Websterian organism. Webster's imagination tends always towards grasping the visual element in an action, and presenting it in a manner that is rich in meaning and in theatrical impact. This constant impulse of the dramatist often attains forms that can be discussed in terms of masque and dumb show, though it cannot be confined to those terms. Dieter

88

Mehl, in *The Elizabethan Dumb Show,* is careful to place Webster's dumb shows in a context of conventions which include "Songs, dances, ceremonial processions, stage properties, and apparitions".[1] We have to do two things here: to concentrate on two categories, masque and dumb show, else the discussion becomes blurred and diffuse; and to be aware of the categories akin to the primary objects of investigation, which reinforce them. I shall touch very lightly upon those adjacent forms that Mehl cites, but otherwise confine myself to the masque and dumb show, in each of the three plays known to be solely Webster's.

I *THE WHITE DEVIL*

The White Devil contains two dumb shows, presented by the Conjurer to show Bracciano the murders of Isabella and Camillo. The stage direction for the first reads:

A dumb show

Enter suspiciously, JULIO *and another, they draw a curtain where* BRACCIANO's *picture is, they put on spectacles of glass, which cover their eyes and noses, and then burn perfumes afore the picture, and wash the lips of the picture, that done, quenching the fire, and putting off their spectacles they depart laughing.*

Enter ISABELLA *in her nightgown as to bed-ward, with lights after her, Count* LODOVICO, GIOVANNI, *and others waiting on her, she kneels down as to prayers, then draws the curtain of the picture, does three reverences to it, and kisses it thrice, she faints and will not suffer them to come near it, dies; sorrow express'd in* GIOVANNI *and in Count* LODOVICO; *she's convey'd out solemnly.* (II. ii)

This is a tiny three-act play in pantomime – preparation for murder, the death of Isabella, the reactions of her retinue. Emotionally, it comprises the laughter of the assassins, the devotion of Isabella, and the grief of Lodovico and Giovanni. The stage dynamics include the pungent odour of the burnt perfumes – I take it the actual performance might well run to this – the candles, and the discreetly erotic effect of Isabella in her nightgown. The meaning of this stage picture is plain enough. As a tableau of poisoning, it identifies a continuing obsession of the play. *Perfume* – an important Websterian word – indicates not only sweetness but the corruption which, as the audience would well know, it was often employed to conceal. ("All the flowers of the spring, / Meet to perfume our burying" was Webster's coding of the idea in *The Devil's Law-Case,* v. iv. 128–9.) But above all, the meaning of this dumb show is concentrated in the centre of its triptych: Isabella, a saint, kisses the icon of her personal God who is her killer. That irony is, of course, later matched by the poisoning of Bracciano, whose "fine embroidered bottles, and perfumes / Equally mortal with a winter plague" become "mercury, and copperas, and quicksilver / With other devilish pothecary stuff / A-melting in your politic brains" (v. iii. 159–63). The idea of *perfume* is a variant on the play's emblematic title.

The second dumb show has much in common with the first. The stage direction reads:

The second dumb show.

Enter FLAMINEO, MARCELLO, CAMILLO, *with four more as Captains, they drink healths and dance; a vaulting-horse is brought into the room;* MARCELLO *and two more whisper'd out of the room while* FLAMINEO *and* CAMILLO *strip themselves into their shirts, as to vault; compliment who shall begin; as* CAMILLO *is about to vault,* FLAMINEO *pitcheth him upon his neck, and with the help of the rest, writhes his neck about, seems to see if it be broke, and lays him folded double as 'twere under the horse, makes shows to call for help;* MARCELLO *come in, laments, sends for the Cardinal* [MONTICELSO] *and Duke* [FRANCISCO], *who comes forth with armed men; wonder at the act;* [FRANCISCO] *commands the body to be carried home, apprehends* FLAMINEO, MARCELLO, *and the rest, and [all] go as 'twere to apprehend* VITTORIA.

Again, let me praise the sheer theatricalism of this incident. No one who saw the Old Vic production (1969) will forget Claude Chagrin's staging of the mimes: the elaborate, courtly exchanges; the unbearably exciting rhythms of a muffled drum, followed by dead silence; the *click,* heard distinctly throughout the theatre, as Flamineo bent back Camillo's neck. The idea remains the same. It is murder, "quaintly done" as Bracciano observes in his oafish way. More, it is murder enveloped in the style and context of a courtly chivalric pastime. Note the *"they drink healths and dance . . . compliment who shall begin"*. I shall return to chivalry later. Here, I stress it as an element in the moral frisson that Webster creates in his audience.

In sum, we have in each dumb show an attack mounted upon our sensibilities, whose sensory impact is in the main visual, but not exclusively so. The baroque synaesthesia here can comprehend the smell of burnt perfume, the sound of music[2] and of the snap of bone. It is an amalgam of beauty – the allure of Court, art, athletic prowess – and death. The meaning points towards a single great *sentential*, the one which Webster used to annotate each of his tragedies:

> Glories, like glow-worms, afar off shine bright
> But look'd to near, have neither heat nor light.
>
> (v. i. 41–2)

It is effectively the epigraph for *The White Devil*.

But the masque: where is the masque in *The White Devil?* There is indeed a glancing allusion in the final scene, Lodovico's "We have brought you a masque" (v. vi. 169), but this is no more than a jest, one which Flamineo caps with "a matachin it seems". More substantial evidence of masque elements is available elsewhere. I propose that we regard in this light the barriers at the beginning of Act v, scene iii. The stage direction reads: *"Charges and shouts. They fight at barriers; first single pairs, then three to three."* "Barriers" is the name of a martial exercise. In it, knights, fight – on horseback, or as here on foot – across a low railing or bar dividing them. For our purposes here, this archaic sport takes on a new life in the Elizabethan revival in the Jacobean age, with its renewed emphasis on chivalric exercises. Above all, "barriers" suggests a specific event, "Prince Henry's Barriers", which took place in January 1610 in the Banqueting House in Whitehall.

Prince Henry's 'Barriers' were both a real martial exercise in which the Prince gave proof of his training in knightly activities, and a theatrical spectacle, or masque, written in verse by Ben Jonson, the theme of which related mythically to the young Prince in a setting designed by Inigo Jones. Two of Jones' existing masque designs belong to the setting for 'Prince Henry's Barriers'.[3]

Frances Yates is exploring a context for Shakespeare, not Webster. However, it seems likely that Webster is drawing on his knowledge of a famous and recent event. (*The White Devil* must have been written between 1610 and 1612.) He is not, I think, making what one would strictly term a topical allusion; and there is of course no parallel between Bracciano and young Prince Henry, whom on the evidence Webster much admired. Rather, he is exploiting audience awareness, and projecting an image of chivalric prowess to which their minds would be fully attuned. And this image, just as the dumb show, contains the meaning of the play. Instead of the knights acting as a prologue to chivalry, they – Lodovico and Francisco, both present at the barriers – instigate a poisoning. The barriers, in providing the spectacle of the poisoner poisoned, figure again the phosphorescent decay of Court allure.

I suggest, then, that Webster is broadly indebted to Prince Henry's Barriers, both as a public event and as a Jonsonian masque (first published in 1608).[4] I shall later consider the structural relation of the masque form to *The White Devil:* but first we have to recognize another variant of Webster's main idea, the spectacular presence of the Ambassadors. They are in Court throughout Vittoria's trial, a body of international and objective observers. Their few utterances are sane, moderate and kind. Webster plays up their visual appeal. Shortly before the trial, this stage direction occurs: "*Here there is a passage of the lieger Ambassadors over the stage severally*" (III. i). Separate entrances are given for the Savoy, French, English and Spanish Ambassadors. Webster does little with the opportunity, beyond giving Flamineo some satirical hits at the French and Spanish Ambassadors. He reserves his main treatment for Act IV, scene iii, when the six Ambassadors appear outside the Pope's palace, where the conclave is taking place. The dialogue runs:

Francisco	Guard well the conclave, and, as the order is,
	Let none have conference with the cardinals.
Lodovico	I shall, my lord: room for the ambassadors, –
Gasparo	They're wondrous brave today: why do they wear
	These several habits?
Lodovico	O sir, they're knights
	Of several orders.
	That lord i'th'black cloak with the silver cross
	Is Knight of Rhodes; the next Knight of S. Michael;

That of the Golden Fleece; the Frenchman there
Knight of the Holy Ghost; my lord of Savoy
Knight of th'Annunciation; the Englishman
Is Knight of th'honoured Garter, dedicated
Unto their saint, S. George. I could describe to you
Their several institutions, with the laws
Annexed to their orders; but that time
Permits not such discovery.

(IV. iii. 2–17)

Again, this takes us back to the territory, though not the words, of Jonson's masque. The first scene in *Prince Henry's Barriers* shows a ruined palace, the Fallen House of Chivalry. The second scene, announced by Merlin, shows the revival of chivalry. It is "St George's Portico", a splendid chapel dedicated to St George.[5] In this superb setting Merlin welcomes Meliadus (that is, Prince Henry), who is to lead and symbolize chivalry's revival. The connection between Lodovico's catalogue of the knights, including St George, and the Jones/Jonson masque setting of St George's Chapel, looks stronger if we take into account Bracciano's later

Your wish is you may leave your warlike swords
For monuments in our chapel. I accept it

(v. i. 50–1)

These traces of indebtedness may be considered mutually corroborative, and the Barriers, like the paraphernalia of chivalry, point to Webster's awareness of the Jonsonian masque.[6]

With the description of the knights, with the papal election and all its panoply, with the fighting at the barriers, we move within the world of ceremonial, of which masque is a crystalline form. But the case for detecting a masque structure does not depend on so general a formulation. Let us return to the main elements of the drama hereabouts, the papal election and the barriers. Webster has carefully written in linking passages, which permit the presence of the Ambassadors at both functions. He gives a speech, whose central importance has I think been neglected, to Bracciano:

You are nobly welcome. We have heard at full
Your honourable service 'gainst the Turk.
To you, brave Mulinassar, we assign

A competent pension: and are inly sorrow
The vows of these two worthy gentlemen
Make them incapable of our proffer'd bounty.
Your wish is you may leave your warlike swords
For monuments in our chapel. I accept it
As a great honour done me, and must crave
Your leave to furnish out our duchess' revels.
Only one thing, as the last vanity
You e'er shall view, deny me not to stay
To see a barriers prepar'd tonight;
You shall have private standings; it hath pleas'd
The great ambassadors of several princes
In their return from Rome to their own countries
To grace our marriage, and to honour me
With such a kind of sport.

(v. i. 44–61)

Not only does "barriers" connote, for Webster's audience, a recent and famous masque; it actually subserves the masque function in this play. The barriers are "to furnish out our duchess' revels": in the presence of the visiting dignitaries, they are "To grace our marriage, and to honour me / With such a kind of sport." The fighting at the beginning of Act v, scene iii, is not a mere affair of blows and thwacks, a routine titillation for the groundlings. It is Webster's masque of chivalry, a martial ritual designed as an entertainment for a Court wedding.

And this masque of chivalry promotes Webster's main idea. Much of these chivalric elements can be taken straight, as sheer theatrical entertainment. Still, the latent reservations and scepticism are always there, waiting to surface. We could, for instance, recall that it is Lodovico, actively involved in the conclave arrangements, who identifies the knights to the audience. The *chef-de-protocole* is an assassin; the mouthpiece of chivalry, who corresponds to the masque's "presenter", is the play's deathsman. Again, even the gorgeous Latin incantation of Arragon's announcement of Monticelso's election is undercut. Latin is the tongue of the fake Franciscans, Gasparo and Lodovico; it is also the fustian rhetoric of the Lawyer at the trial. (The association of Latin with the Devil is explicit in ii. ii. 19–20.) The impression given is of corrupt splendour, tainted pomp. And the formal purpose of Bracciano's wedding entertainment is inverted by the assassins. The world of the masque is subverted from within, by its own practitioners. It is tempting to say that in viewing a masque we effectively perceive an antimasque: but that would stretch the meaning of antimasque so far as to make it virtually a metaphor. And we need "antimasque" to describe a precisely circumscribed operation in *The Duchess of Malfi.* Let us say, then, that the masque elements in *The White Devil* compose a parody masque. The masquers betray their own tradition. They are imbued with the spirit of irony that dominates the entire piece.

II *THE DUCHESS OF MALFI*

The Duchess of Malfi exhibits a diminished interest in dumb show, and a heightened awareness of the possibilities of assimilating masque to drama. The reasons are fairly clear. Dumb show is a technical device which, however powerful in impact, finds difficulty in expressing more than its immediate content. It is a species of intensely concentrated literal statement, if you like. But masque has an exterior life of its own, with its own moral ecology. When alluded to in drama, it creates infinite reverberations. It belongs to the mode of symbolic statement. Webster again found the masque well adapted to his artistic purposes, and he built Act IV around it. Before I turn to the masque, however, I shall dispose of the play's solitary dumb show. It occurs in Act III, scene iv, at the Shrine of Our Lady of Loretto:

> *Here the ceremony of the* Cardinal's *instalment in the habit of a soldier, performed in delivering up his cross, hat, robes and ring at the shrine, and investing him with sword, helmet, shield and spurs; then* ANTONIO, *the* Duchess *and their* Children, *having presented themselves at the shrine, are (by a form of banishment in dumb show expressed towards them by the cardinal and the state of Ancona) banished: during all which ceremony, this ditty is sung, to very solemn music, by divers* Churchmen; *and then exeunt* [*all, except the Two Pilgrims*].

Obviously, the instalment of the Cardinal parallels the papal election of *The White Devil,* and it figures the same idea of corruption under the show of ceremony, both religious and chivalric. It is a technically useful telescoping of the action, and it affords an opportunity for solemn music, though as it happens the words are of stunning banality. ("The author disclaims this ditty to be his" runs the marginal note: as well he might, says Lucas.) However, Webster is simply repeating his effects here, and the episode does not call for protracted commentary. Nor does the waxwork horror show, a dumb show of sorts. Webster's main imaginative effort is reserved for Act IV, and the episode of the madmen is of particular concern to us.

Act IV, in the play's design, is the response to Act I. The Duchess's initiative in wooing and wedding Antonio leads to her prolonged torture and death in Act IV. In Act I, the Duchess and Antonio compose an invocation to Heaven, which is a hymn to order and harmony:

> *Duchess*   Bless, heaven, this sacred Gordian, which let violence
>   Never untwine.
> *Antonio*   And may our sweet affections, like the spheres,
>   Be still in motion.
> *Duchess*   Quickening, and make
>   The like soft music.
> *Antonio*   That we may imitate the loving palms,
>   Best emblem of a peaceful marriage,
>   That ne'er bore fruit, divided.
>
> (I. i. 480–7)

It appears as the fragment of a private masque, staged before heaven and a human audience of one. On it the Duchess, with a detectable change of tone, comments "What can the church force more?" But that same human audience, Cariola, has this at the scene's end:

> Whether the spirit of greatness or of woman
> Reign most in her, I know not, but it shows
> A fearful madness. I owe her much of pity.
>
> (I. i. 504–6)

The formal inversion occurs in Act IV, scene ii, with the entry of the madmen. Their role is to make physical "a fearful madness." It is now generally recognized[7] that the madmen present an antimasque, a grotesquerie which distorts or inverts the major themes of the masque. On it, John Russell Brown comments:

By using this well-known form, Webster ensured that his audience would receive the song of howling and death, the bawdy, devil-ridden, and competitive dialogue and the fantastic dance as expressions of the duchess' situation as well as instruments of Ferdinand's cruelty; they would know that, somehow, she had to accept or control this lewd, egocentric, and doomed world. The dance would be the climax of the episode, a concerted expression of uncontrolled 'wildness' (cf. 1. 41). The audience would also expect the masque proper to follow. Bosola's disguises as 'tomb-maker' and 'common bellman' carry this expectation forward, and soon he delivers a 'present' of *'coffin, cords and a bell'* in a 'presence-chamber' (1. 171), accompanying this with a formal speech. So far Webster continued within the masque form, and he accentuated the correspondence by making Bosola's dirge echo such an epithalamium as Jonson provided in his *Hymenaei*.[8]

The dirge, as Brown notes, is at several points antithetical to the epithalamium. The distinction that I wish to emphasize here is between the antimasque, which relates only to the appearance of the "franticks", and the parody masque, which comprises the larger sense of presence chamber, ritual, and inverted epithalamium. Within this schema of antimasque embedded in parody masque, certain details are available for performance and are worth canvassing. I have proposed elsewhere[9] that the identities of the first four madmen are suggestively close to four of the major dramatis personae. The madmen are listed as

> a mad lawyer, and a secular priest,
> A doctor that hath forfeited his wits
> By jealousy; an astrologian
> That in his works said such a day o'th'month
> Should be the day of doom, and failing of't,
> Ran mad
>
> (IV. ii. 45–50)

The astrologian sounds like an analogue to Bosola, that star-gazing scholar. The secular priest is the Cardinal. The doctor recalls the charlatan who fails to cure Ferdinand, and the lawyer is Ferdinand himself, who in Act I is presented as a judge and in Act IV explicitly renounces that role: "was I her judge?" (IV. ii. 299). It's a neat schema, which has some inviting implications for performance, especially if the speaking parts are shuffled somewhat.[10] However, we can make perfectly good sense of the episode by concentrating on what the madmen say, not who they are. "Reason in madness" has always to be taken seriously in Jacobean drama. The themes of the madmen are hell and damnation, medicine, heraldry, Puritanism, sleep. Now these topics are touched on, more or less obsessively, elsewhere in the play, and the madmen thus become a series of animated gargoyles, mopping and mouthing at ideas taken seriously elsewhere. Much of the reference is designedly loose. For instance, consider

> *1st Madman*   I have skill in heraldry.
> *2nd Madman*   Hast?
> *1st Madman*   You do give for your crest a woodcock's head, with the brains picked out on't – you are a very ancient gentleman.
>
> (IV. ii. 86–90)

The audience can take this as picking up Bosola's "Will you make yourself a mercenary herald, / Rather to examine men's pedigrees than virtues?" (III. ii. 259–60). Or it may, equally, regard the passage as satire on Ferdinand and the Cardinal, with their crazed idea of "honour". The heraldry racket had in any case been a public scandal for years.[11] It is theatre of hints, of suggestions that reach out towards the major dramatis personae, and beyond them. One feature of the antimasque's design is, as one would expect, marked: the madmen's dialogue reads like a reversal of much that is in the earlier miniature masque. So "love", for the Duchess and Antonio, becomes lechery, a hand in a wench's placket. The "cure" for Antonio's bloodshot eye becomes the placebo of rogue apothecaries. The "heaven" whose blessing the lovers solicit becomes the "hell" of the madmen, which augments the experiential hell of the Duchess, "this sensible hell". Such direct and schematic inversions link the madmen's discourse with the harmonies of the private wedding, and thus clarify the contours of the antimasque.

We might go further, and look for the antimasque's meaning as being especially accessible in the utterance of one madman (whose identity here is unclear: it may be the doctor):

> Woe to the caroche, that brought home my wife from the masque, at three o'clock in the morning! it had a large featherbed in it. (IV. ii. 104–6)

Since the word "masque" does actually occur here, the passage is worth pausing over. One has to consider not only what the term means, but what it symbolizes. "Masque" is not simply a court entertainment, whose values are confirmed by the approval of the speaker, and which may be phrased in some glowing formulation:

> Such a combining of dynasty and fancy and moralizing expresses the highest aspirations of a humanist society, the partnership of power and culture in a sententious and joyful entertainment.[12]

That is a way of looking at it, and no doubt many onlookers would have seen it that way. But "masque" could also be viewed as something approximating to a type of luxury, and it is to that type that the madman refers. It encodes the ideas of revelling and wantonness in high places, as well as the formal disciplines and values of the masque production itself. This comes out vividly in *The Revenger's Tragedy*. Antonio's description of his wife's rape is framed thus:

> Last revelling night,
> When torchlight made an artificial noon
> About the court, some courtiers in the masque,
> Putting on better faces that their own,
> Being full of fraud and flattery –
> > (I. iv. 26–30, Revels Plays edn)

Vindice tempts his mother thus:

> O, think upon the pleasure of the palace;
> Secured ease and state; the stirring meats,
> Ready to move out of the dishes, that
> E'en now quicken when they're eaten;
> Banquets abroad by torchlight, music, sports
> > (II. i. 199–203)

Viewed from this angle, the masque focuses all that is most alluring and most corrupt at Court. As M. C. Bradbrook has written, "when masques are dramatically depicted in the plays of this period, they tend to reflect the public distrust of the form".[13]

We need this promenade around "masque" to get at the status of "antimasque" in *The Duchess of Malfi*. "Antimasque", obviously, is not a true opposite to "masque". It is purely an apt and striking challenge, which is put up to be put down. The forces of moral law and order make an effective demonstration of their power to quell the dissident voices. The statement made in *The Duchess of Malfi* is altogether different. Webster is fully aware of the dark and sceptical view of "masque" current at this period, and he goes beyond mere social satire to project, in Act IV, the appalling possibility that is, I think, easily available in dramatic practice: that the antimasque is the core of this play's experience, that chaos is the original state to which society tends, and against which the fictions of order un-availingly contend.

That is why it is, I think, misleading to call the Duchess's private marriage a "defection from Degree"; "far from endorsing ceremony and the values it represents, the Duchess engages in a profane parody, employing the ritual solemnities of Degree to confirm and sanction the autonomy of private impulse".[14] Degree, in this read-ing, is the norm from which the Duchess departs. That passage was written before the full reaction against *The Elizabethan World Picture* had occurred. Nowadays, I suppose, one wonders more and more if offences against Degree were ever really on the statute book: in the drama of the early seventeenth century, at all events. What emerges from the madmen episode is not a sense of Degree infringed, but a profound scepticism directed at the world of ceremony itself.

How is this sense of masque and antimasque translated into the language of theatre? The initial problem for a modern audience is that it is without experience of masque, and the director must find his own way to the truth of the episode. He has several possibilities. Clifford Williams, in the RSC production of 1971, kept in touch with the comic aspects of madness. The *Shakespeare Survey* reviewer felt that this detracted from their menace: "The madmen were not farcical, but they were frivolous."[15] In the same year, Jean Gascon's production at Stratford, Ontario, reached out towards the associa-tions of *Marat/Sade*. These were genuine lunatics, who wore night-shirts and projected a terrifying dementia. Here, surely, is the classic frisson of the scene, the last outpost of sanity threatened by the waves of attackers. But there is another way of presenting the madmen episode, and tying it to the masque tradition. As John Russell Brown has pointed out,[16] one of the unifying devices of *The Duchess of Malfi* is the presence-chamber: it is the milieu of several scenes in which she appears. The reversals and transformations which take place within the felt context of the presence-chamber

create, and reinforce, the meaning of the drama. I am indebted to
Alexander Leggatt for an account of a production at the University
of Toronto Drama Centre's Studio Theatre, which seized on this
aspect of the matter:

> In this production, certain masque suggestions were present
> throughout Act IV, but were clearest in the madmen episode. The
> Act was played by candlelight (the only part of the play that
> was); a large candelabrum was lit, one candle at a time, at the
> end. The Duchess was given a chair centre-stage (the only chair
> used in the production) and hardly ever moved from it. The other
> characters (except the madmen) were plainly dressed, but she
> had a rich dark silver dress that caught the candlelight. The effect
> was of the Prince sitting in the centre of her world while various
> 'shows' were presented to her.
>
> The madmen wore masks with elaborate headdresses, and
> fancy court costumes, one of which suggested a court fool. On
> their entrance they did a slow march, two by two, down the
> centre aisle through the audience, singing the dirge. Their
> speeches were delivered from formal postures, in a stylized way.
> There was no attempt to suggest actual madness; rather, gro-
> tesque comedy acting, and this seemed to work well with their
> speeches as written. Their dance was a formal court dance gone a
> bit wrong; one of the madmen attempted to take Cariola out and
> dance with her, but she fought him off.
>
> During the dance, Bosola as the Bellman did a slow circling
> cross around the back of the stage. Appearing at the front, he had
> the effect of scattering the madmen, who fled through the audi-
> ence. This was, as it were, the end of the antimasque. The
> Bellman wore a long black cloak with a plain white mask; the
> solitary executioner wore the traditional black mask. When he
> and Bosola were alone with the Duchess, for the strangling, the
> effect of the three figures was emblematic: the Prince and the two
> ambassadors of death. The general effect was that the usual
> machinery of court ceremony was being used, this time not to
> celebrate the Prince but to torment and destroy her.[17]

I quote this account at length because it is a fine instance of the
strategy of using stage performance as a test for interpretation. The
account demonstrates that "antimasque" can be projected successfully to a modern audience, and in such a way as to illuminate

Webster's intention: the grave questioning of "ceremony" and all it stands for.

That is at the heart of *The Duchess of Malfi*'s meaning, a play, uniquely, whose human centre has no name, only a title. It does not concern us here to consider the answers to the questioning Webster arrives at, to pursue the implications of "I am Duchess of Malfi still" and Bosola's dying speech. Suffice it to note that shortly after the exit of the madmen Bosola speaks, to the Duchess, the same *sententia* that hangs over *The White Devil*: "*Glories, like glow-worms, afar off shine bright, / But look'd to near, have neither heat, nor light*" (IV. ii. 144–5). The point emerges with greater structural force than in *The White Devil*. The antimasque in *Thè Duchess of Malfi* is the great engine of challenge to "the glories of our blood and state".

III   *THE DEVIL'S LAW-CASE*

The Devil's Law-Case is a modified and revised version of the statement Webster makes in the two great tragedies. The adjustments of tone and mood do not indicate an outlook essentially different from that detectable in the tragedies, and certain devices – which include masque and dumb shows – are again employed. The play is an anthology of genres, but for most of its course is a satiric comedy, one which concentrates on the class tensions between the nobility and moneyed interests. The terrain is formally Naples, effectively Jacobean England; this is an exposé of a society whose representatives struggle ceaselessly for money and social status, and who at the end are punished largely by fines – which they can well afford. Law infringed is the theme of this play, and that on three levels – divine (or "supreme") law, civil law, and natural law. If there is an emotional core to *The Devil's Law-Case*, it occurs in the trial scene, with Romelio's passionate outburst against the world of state and power, and its essential illegitimacy:

> Yet why do I
> Take bastardy so distastefully, when i'th'world
> A many things that are essential parts
> Of greatness are but by-slips, and are father'd
> On the wrong parties?
> Preferment in the world a many times
> Basely begotten? Nay, I have observ'd

> The immaculate justice of a poor man's cause,
> In such a court as this, has not known whom
> To call father, which way to direct itself
> For compassion –
>
> (IV. ii. 329–39)

"Bastardy" is Webster's metaphor for disorder and wrong in society. With Romelio's outcry we can link Crispiano's quieter, reflective

> We observe
> Obedience of creatures to the law of Nature
> Is the stay of the whole world; here that law is broke,
> For though our civil law makes difference
> 'Tween the base and the legitimate,
> Compassionate Nature makes them equal, nay,
> She many times prefers them.
>
> (IV. ii. 263–9)

The Hooker lines have the force less of borrowing, than of direct reference or quotation. It is an elegy for the world we have lost, a lament for the passing of a vision of natural decency not incompatible with the formal requirements of the civil order. Hooker is the past (the passage cited appeared in 1594), the great coding of a set of standards impossible to detect in the society of 1617. Most of the dramatis personae here are etched with an acid that expresses, surely, Webster's revulsion with the society of his day. It is venal, heartless, given over to the pursuit of wealth and status. At the play's end Ariosto, the impotent Judge, is left to swallow his rage, compel his hearers to what minor reparations lie within his power, and sourly contemplate an outcome "with success beyond our wishes crowned". The play is Webster's *The Way We Live Now*.

The dumb show and masque elements occur in the crisis of Act v. As the Capuchin finishes preparing Romelio's soul for the combat, Leonora enters, and a dumb show ensues (v. iv):

> *Enter* Leonora, *with two coffins borne by her servants, and two winding-sheets stuck with flowers; presents one to her son, and the other to* Julio.

To this, Romelio responds "'Tis very welcome", then breaks into the loveliest of Webster's elegies: "All the flowers of the spring / Meet to perfume our burying." This "dumb pageant", as Romelio calls it, is not like those present in the tragedies. It has no narrative content, and does not represent the telescoping of action. The "pageant" has purely emblematic status. It seems almost as if Leonora perceives herself as the participant in a masque. The grave, ritualized beauty of this passage is transformed as Romelio tricks his mother and the Capuchin into the closet. So the "right excellent form of penitence" it expresses is reversed in the immediate sequel. Nevertheless the dumb show is an elegiac grace-note on "courts adieu".

It is followed by the combat. Here Webster reverts to the mode of chivalric allusion, which he had used so extensively in *The White Devil,* and in the matter of horsemanship touched on in *The Duchess of Malfi.* I quote the opening of the final scene:

> *The lists set up. Enter the* Marshal, Crispiano, *and* Ariosto, *as Judges; they sit.* [*With them,* Sanitonella, *attendants, and* Herald.]

Marshal	Give the appellant his summons; do the like To the defendant.

> *Two tuckets by several trumpets. Enter at one door,* Ercole *and* Contarino; *at the other,* Romelio *and* Julio.

	Can any of you allege aught why the combat should not proceed?
Combatants	Nothing.
Ariosto	Have the knights weighed And measured their weapons?
Marshal	They have.
Ariosto	Proceed, then, to the battle, and may heaven Determine the right!
Herald	*Soit la bataille, et victoire à ceux qui ont droit.*

(v. vi. 1–8)

Romelio, bidding an attendant fetch the Capuchin, cries "Victoire, à ceux qui ont droit", to which *All The Champ* (or "field of battle") cry, with satisfying unanimity, "Victoire à ceux qui ont droit!"

How are we to take all this? Much the same point can be made here as on the barriers in *The White Devil.* For those who like their Wardour Street neat, no comment is required. This is routine swashbuckling, and the stage direction, *The combat continued to a good length,* tells all. For those who, additionally, care to think about the meaning of these chivalric war-cries, the text is a nonsense. How can "Victoire à ceux qui ont droit" possibly relate to a combat in which Romelio and that shifty opportunist, Contarino, are on opposite sides? It is impossible to resolve the action through the dramatic means initiated: the quadruple duel is a spectacular destined to end in moral failure. All the playwright can do is to stop the contest. And this he does through the entrance of Leonora and the Capuchin. Explanations follow, and Ariosto's disgusted "How insolently has this high Court of Honour / Been abused" (v. vi. 28–9) sums up this phase of the action.

Then follows the final phase, in which the action reverts to the mode of masque:

> *Enter* Angiolella *veil'd and* Jolenta, *her face colour'd like a Moor; the two Surgeons, one of them like a Jew.*

Ariosto	How, now, who are these?
Second Surgeon	A couple of strange fowl, and I the falconer
	That have sprung them. This is a white nun
	Of the order of Saint Clare; and this a black one,
	You'll take my word for't.

> *Discovers* Jolenta.

Ariosto	She's a black one, indeed.
Jolenta	Like or dislike me, choose you whether:
	The down upon the raven's feather
	Is as gentle and as sleek
	As the mole on Venus' cheek.
	Hence, vain show! I only care
	To preserve my soul most fair;
	Never mind the outward skin,
	But the jewel that's within;
	And though I want the crimson blood,
	Angels boast my sisterhood.
	Which of us now judge you whiter,
	Her whose credit proves the lighter,
	Or this black and ebon hue,
	That, unstained, keeps fresh and true?
	For I proclaim't without control,
	There's no true beauty but i'th'soul.

(v. vi. 29–49)

A strange entrance, this: it seems to have no purpose beyond offering a visual and moral paradox, culminating in "There's no true beauty, but i'th'soul". Jolenta's explanation, that she was running away from the combat, is her last utterance. The entrance seems a reminiscence of Jonson's *Masque of Blackness* (1605) in which, it will be recalled, Queen Anne appeared as a negress, one of the twelve daughters of the Niger. Dudley Carleton left an account of the performance:

> Their Apparell was rich, but too light and Curtizan-like for such great ones. Instead of Vizzards, their Faces and Arms up to the Elbows were painted black, which was Disguise sufficient, for they were hard to be known; *but it became them nothing so well as their red and white, and you cannot imagine a more ugly Sight, then a Troop of lean-cheek'd Moors.* The *Spanish* and *Venetian* Ambassadors were both present. . . . [The Spanish Ambassador] took out the Queen, and forgot not to kiss her Hand, though there was Danger it would have left a Mark on his Lips.[18]

Moreover, there are parallels between the verbal imagery of Jonson's masque and Jolenta's speech. The opening song of *The Masque of Blackness* invokes "Fair Niger":

> With all his beauteous race,
> Who, though but black in face,
> Yet are they bright,
> And full of life and light
> To prove that beauty best
> Which not the colour but the feature
> Assures unto the creature.
>
> (II. 88–94)[19]

"The central conceit of *The Masque of Blackness*", as Meagher remarks,[20] "is that the daughters of Niger, the masquers, are beautiful despite their blackness." Broadly, this is Webster's conceit too, though his handling of it is not identical: Jonson goes on to attribute their blackness to the sun, the source of light:

> Though he – the best judge and most formal cause
> Of all dames' beauties – in their firm hues draws
> Signs of his fervent'st love, and thereby shows
> That in their black the perfect'st beauty grows
>
> (II. 123–6)

Webster prefers to stay with the static paradox of "outward skin", "no true beauty, but i'th'soul". A further point: Webster's debt is to the *Masque of Blackness*, whose "ultimate resolution is achieved only in a sequel, *The Masque of Beautie*".[21] Orgel suggests that we think of these two works as standing to each other as antimasque to masque. This, for us, emphasizes our need to think of the antimasque as a recurring device in Webster's theatre.

Jolenta's speech seems purely gestural, a mere allusion. It has no bearing on the action, which is peremptorily stilled by the sentences Ariosto hands down. Are we, then, to regard the masque here as part of a general artistic failure? In the absence of any stage performance, which might guide our interpretation, I suggest that we look at matters more positively. Suppose we see the finale as a study in disintegration: this permits us to regard dumb show, chivalric contest, and masque as purely gestures, signifying nothing and leading nowhere. The moral centre of the play is a recognition that the centre cannot hold. The concern with "law" – divine, civil and natural – is Webster's threnody on "degree".

Indeed, the standard comparison between the endings of *The Devil's Law-Case* and *Measure for Measure* – by reason of the sentences handed down, and those portions of the action which, owing to the lack of collateral instruction, must be determined in performance – seems to me something less than fully perceptive. The precedent that matters is *Troilus and Cressida*. *The Devil's Law-Case* has the same sour taste of curdled chivalry, the trappings of a glittering past that fail to relate to, or resolve, the present. The language of the contestants here, the Herald's Norman-French, recalls *Troilus and Cressida*. As David Horowitz observes, "The language of Paris' question ('noble', 'faith', 'true') is the language of the ghost order of value that haunts this world and conflicts so violently with its reality."[22] The mediaevalism, the conscious archaism of *Troilus and Cressida* is one of Shakespeare's subtlest strategies to identify the inner nature of the action. So here. We now see Ulysses' "degree" cadenza very differently from Tillyard; but however one sees it, it remains at the core of a play which dramatizes disintegration. Webster's play is about the collapse of order, and the terrifying inadequacy of the rickety structure Ariosto erects at the end. It is a statement that combines revulsion and contempt, a Happy End that suggests the collaboration, not of Beaumont and Fletcher, but of Brecht and Weill.

Webster's final placing of masque and dumb show, then, is

within a context which they fail to grip. The progression from disorder to order that is the thematic idea of the masque[23] undergoes an original transposition: the ostensible imposition of order is itself a recognition of ungovernable disorder. So the association of stage masque with ironic intent – an association that begins with *The Maid's Tragedy* (1610) and culminates in *A Tale of a Tub* (1633) – is, as I take it, present here.[24]

To conclude. Drama converts everything to its own uses, and the Court masque takes on with Webster individual resonances. Dumb show is an essentially technical stage form; it is purely a department of dramatic expressionism. But the Court masque takes with it a structure of social, political, and theological values. It is a total system. In assimilating it to his theatrical purposes, Webster makes, necessarily by implication, a statement concerning that system. The statement is one of challenge and subversion. Now the problem for the playwright of genius is this: how does one use the masque to challenge the world of the masque? Clearly, what the masque world designates as "antimasque" is no kind of answer. The words associated with antimasque, "foil", "preposterous", "fantastic", and so on, tell all. "Antimasque", in the accepted sense, is merely a mechanical challenge, tokenism if you like, which is absorbed into the main tenor of the "masque" statement. So the playwright's art must find other solutions. Webster's preferred device is the parody masque – or inverted masque – and in this context, his antimasque does indeed assume a terrifying reality. The challenge has become genuine. And in all three plays Webster's imagination, as I conceive it, grasps for means of challenging the propositions of order, hierarchy, and ceremony. Webster's statement is highly individual; but formally, one discerns more clearly through the masque elements the outlines of one of Webster's great, and acknowledged influences, "the labour'd and understanding works of Master Jonson".

8 Shakespeare and Chivalry

"My kingdom for a horse." Richard *in extremis* needs a horse for power, mobility, continued existence. That is what horses are for in *Richard III,* to enable *cavalry* – the horse-owning class – to ride over opposition. No other values emerge, however attenuated. It is a brutal play on the climax of a brutal era. But other plays in the Histories show the beginnings of Shakespeare's fascination with chivalry – by which I mean a code of values, a standard of honour and knighthood, derived at bottom from the possession of a horse. The concept cannot however be illustrated by the mere act of photographing horse and rider in vivid action. Chivalry is Shakespeare's subtlest anachronism. It is always against ("back in") time. Merely by naming chivalry, one is drawn towards acknowledging that people do not display it, towards investing the word with irony or regret.[1] Chivalry, as a stage fact, is itself a kind of enamel, a glamorized coating of men and events with the colours and trappings of knighthood. It serves to identify a defunct ideology. Chivalry is the costume drama of the mind, and Shakespeare touches on it at many points before his great and definitive treatment in *Troilus and Cressida.*

Why should he be impelled to write of chivalry at all? The revival of chivalry, in the later years of Elizabeth's reign, must surely have acted on Shakespeare's mind. The tournaments and Accession Day tilts, of which Frances Yates writes,[2] were recurring public celebrations of chivalry. Court spectacle and pageantry proclaimed chivalric values. No mere cult, this revival had its roots in reasons of state. Frances Yates views it as "an imaginative re-feudalization of culture", and as a European phenomenon: its true function was to support the monarchies, "which used the apparatus of chivalry and its religious traditions to focus fervent religious loyalty on the national monarch".[3] Shakespeare, however, treats chivalry as largely detached from the immediate political process (though there are suggestive undertones in *Richard II*). For him, chivalry is less a political exercise than an interesting growth in the human mind.

His fascination is with chivalry as a value-system in decay. It promotes values of the highest worth, yet fails to sustain them; ultimately it collapses into organized posturing, an ideology of unreality. Chivalry, like all else in Shakespeare, must stand the audit of time.

These considerations are social and general, however much they apply to individuals. The key instance is the Earl of Essex. With some reservation, I incline to accept the well-known linking of Essex with Achilles, in *Troilus and Cressida*. It is generally, I think, a mistake to read any one of Shakespeare's characters (excluding historical personages) as a simple equivalent of a known human being. Shakespeare's imagination works to decompose the individual, then to reconstitute him in dramatically appropriate forms. Still, Essex is an outstanding candidate for reconstitution; and the formal link, which G. B. Harrison first pointed out,[4] is undeniable. Chapman's translation of Homer, published in 1598, is dedicated "To the most honoured now living instance of the Achillean virtues eternized by divine Homer, the Earl of Essex, Earl Marshal, etc." Campbell's phrasing of Harrison's view, "that Shakespeare, when writing *Troilus and Cressida,* could not have dissociated Achilles from Essex, nor could his audience have done so",[5] seems to me exactly right. What that gives us, however, is not a *drame à clef.* Essex emerges as a focus of contemplation, one who actually did embody to excess the chivalric values, and carried them well past the border of sanity. Lytton Strachey catches him before Lisbon: "Into one of the gates of the town Essex, as a parting gesture, thrust his pike, 'demanding aloud if any Spaniard mewed therein durst adventure forth in favour of his mistress to break a lance.' There was no reply".[6] It is like *Troilus and Cressida,* "No trumpet answers." In the following year, 1591, Essex while at the siege of Rouen challenged the enemy's commander, Villars, to single combat. There is no need to reject the virtual certainty of Essex's presence in Shakespeare's mind, as a supreme instance of a type. It is that type, from the second tetralogy to *Troilus and Cressida,* that occupies so much of Shakespeare's gaze.

I

The early histories do no more than touch an allusion. In *1 Henry VI,* Talbot addresses his son John on the battlefield, "Now art thou seal'd the son of chivalry" (IV. vi. 29). There is no irony apparent, yet the play requires us to think of the valiant limitations of Talbot; certainly there is little disposition today among commentators to view Talbot as the "Hero" of Part One. In *3 Henry VI*, Clifford's murder of young Rutland is reduced, for Edward, to "Thou hast slain / The flow'r of Europe for his chivalry" (II. i. 70–1). The note is purely elegiac. These early allusions are markers for the ironic and elegiac treatments which Shakespeare is later to develop. A more extended analysis appears in *Richard II*.

The chivalric is the given mode of the opening. The conflict between Bolingbroke and Mowbray, couched in the language of knightly assertion, emerges as

> *Bolingbroke*   Pale trembling coward, there I throw my gage,
>   Disclaiming here the kindred of the King,
>   And lay aside my high blood's royalty,
>   Which fear, not reverence, makes thee to except.
>   If guilty dread have left thee so much strength
>   As to take up mine honour's pawn, then stoop.
>   By that, and all the rites of knighthood else,
>   Will I make good against thee, arm to arm,
>   What I have spoke, or thou canst worse devise.
> *Mowbray*   I take it up; and by that sword I swear,
>   Which gently laid my knighthood on my shoulder,
>   I'll answer thee in any fair degree
>   Or chivalrous design of knightly trial;
>   And when I mount, alive may I not light,
>   If I be traitor or unjustly fight!
>
>   (I. i. 69–83)

Challenge, counter-challenge, hostilities decorously channelled into ritual in the King's presence: this is the open and acceptable face of chivalry, and it is approved of by the King himself: "we shall see / Justice design the victor's chivalry" (I. i. 202–3). The mode is intensified in the Coventry tournament that follows (I. iii), with its apparatus of lists, Marshals, trumpets, and its talk of champions and appellants. Theatrically, the build up to the combat is formal and impressive. The chivalric subserves the needs of ritual:

> *King Richard*   Marshal, ask yonder knight in arms
>   Both who he is and why he cometh hither

	Thus plated in habiliments of war,
	And formally, according to our law,
	Depose him in the justice of his cause.
Marshal	What is thy name? And wherefore com'st thou hither,
	Before King Richard in his royal lists?
	Against whom comest thou? And what's thy quarrel?
	Speak like a true knight, so defend thee heaven!

(I. iii. 26–34)

And yet, the dramatic point of all this preparation turns out to be anti-climax. The knightly combat will not take place. Richard, for good if undisclosed reasons of state, throws down his baton ("warder"), and stops the contest. It is not hard to infer that Richard views the survival of either combatant as a political disaster; hence a dual exit is the best solution. Still, the play refuses to explore the motives, the historical foundations, the true *raison d'état* of the tournament. After all, the focus of the play is elsewhere, on the mind of the King and of Bolingbroke. So the chivalric glitter of Act I, scenes i and iii, creates a curiously oblique impression, a swirl of surface activity at some remove from the inner movements of State. The theatrical key, the device waiting for *Troilus and Cressida,* is the linking of chivalry with anti-climax.

Richard II shows the demands of power breaking through, or thrusting aside, the forms and language of loyal fealty. Clearly, chivalry, which is the image of a hierarchic and ordered world, is unable to cope with the brutal exigences of politics and foundering authority. It is not designed to. No Arthur, no chivalry. The course of the play invests with additional poignancy John of Gaunt's vision of an England renowned "For Christian service and *true* chivalry" (II. i. 54). The real, not the ersatz version is his point. By the end of Act v the events of Act I have taken on the status of a failed ideology, the flickering lamps of a vanished world.

Hence it is dramatically apt that Henry IV, in the plays that follow, does not attempt to rekindle the lamp of chivalry. He has problems enough in merely surviving, in asserting what authority he can over his mutinous vassals. And how can Bolingbroke utter the ancient words of power? It is Hal who acknowledges the mode, not his father. "I have a truant been to chivalry" (*1 Henry IV,* v. i.

94). More, Vernon's admiring account of Hal and his followers offers an intense, glowing image of knightly prowess:

> all furnish'd, all in arms;
> All plum'd like estridges, that with the wind
> Bated like eagles having lately bath'd,
> Glittering in golden coats, like images
> As full of spirit as the month of May
> And gorgeous as the sun at midsummer;
> Wanton as youthful goats, wild as young bulls.
> I saw young Harry, with his beaver on,
> His cushes on his thighs, gallantly arm'd,
> Rise from the ground like feathered Mercury,
> And vaulted with such ease into his seat
> As if an angel dropp'd down from the clouds
> To turn and wind a fiery Pegasus
> And witch the world with noble horsemanship.
>
> (IV. i. 97–110)

There is no apparent irony here whatsoever. Vernon has nothing but whole-hearted praise for the young Prince. But the context is the play, not the scene. The scene that follows, starring Falstaff, is an unmistakable pairing. Act IV, scenes i and ii, offer a diptych of war: one panel, painted by Vernon, portrays the glamour and idealism of young aristocrats for whom *horsemanship* is a focus of knightly values; the other panel is painted by Falstaff (on foot) in his sardonic audience-address of IV. ii. 11–47. Falstaff presents war as an affair for the poor, the unemployed, criminals and dropouts; those who can afford to, pay to dodge the draft. It is a devastating, unanswerable, and permanent statement of reality, one which dislodges Vernon's romanticism from the mind. Chivalry, linked with anti-climax in *Richard II*, is in *1 Henry IV* refuted by juxtaposition.

Chivalry has no place in *2 Henry IV*, Prince John's world, and it finds only the elegy of Lady Percy for her dead husband:

> and by his light
> Did all the chivalry of England move
> To do brave acts.
>
> (II. iii. 19–21)

That is it, a plain statement of values upheld by the dead, and self-evidently unequal to the complex and demanding world in which his conqueror (and his sense of "honour") survives. It is as though Shakespeare must always swing between the poles of irony and elegy, as he contemplates chivalry. In *Henry V* it was the turn of irony.

There is no need to argue here for the ironic reading of *Henry V*. The darker elements of the play are the shadows of the Ideal King. The Council scene reference to chivalry, "When all her [England's] chivalry hath been in France" (I. ii. 157), is spoken by Canterbury as he gilds the English invasion of France. No value escapes intact from Canterbury's support. But here again, as in *1 Henry IV,* Shakespeare speaks in the language of parallel and caricature. For a sceptical presentation of chivalry we must turn to the French. It is they who project most vividly the aura of chivalry,[7] and we can catch at Shakespeare's drift through the iteration of *cheval*. It is the Dauphin's word: it would be. "Le cheval volant, the Pegasus!" (III. vii. 14) is a sampling of the Dauphin's paean to his horse, a paean which in the ensuing dialogue is reduced to a series of jokes on bestiality. The Dauphin's disquisition on his horse parodies chivalry as savagely as anything in *Troilus and Cressida*. Yet the Dauphin is calling "Montez à cheval! My horse, varlet lackey! Ha!" (IV. ii. 2) as Agincourt dawns. The Dauphin is Henry's foil; and we can note his tinsel language here, with French – the sort of schoolboy French that almost everybody can take in – used to destroy the pretensions of chivalric gesture. (The English is purest Wardour Street. The "varlet lackey" and "Ha!" are particularly neat touches.) On the English stage, the French language easily subverts its own speakers. All is set up, then, for the broad openness of Act IV, scene iv, when the two greatest cowards in the French and English armies find each other, by a happy instinct, and the language of chivalry governs Monsieur Le Fer's capitulation: "je m'estime heureux que je suis tombé entre les mains d'un chevalier" (IV. iv. 57–8). Pistol, a chevalier: it does rather affect one's view of chevaliers.

And yet one cannot leave it there, nor does the play. The dying York's farewell to Suffolk, "We kept together in our chivalry" (IV. vi. 19), escapes irony. So, I think, does the Constable of France, and with him the best elements of the French court. (It is an established truth of stage history that *Henry V*'s scenes at the French court need to be played with warmth and respect.) And so does Montjoy. The French Herald, noble in mien and language, is in no way impeached by the play. Shakespeare grants a full respect to France's diplomatic representative, and to the values he guards. We should remember Montjoy when we consider the Trojan Herald, Aeneas.

The Histories present, as they must, a portfolio of Shakespeare's sketches of chivalry. I pass over the affectionate and oddly touching miniature he supplies in *The Two Gentlemen of Verona*, Sir Eglamour. A charming (and traditionally, elderly) representative of the old school, Sir Eglamour, for all his protestations of knightly service, escorts Silvia to the forest – then runs away out of trouble. Many actors and audiences have enjoyed their brief acquaintance with Sir Eglamour – chivalry, as Shakespeare knew early, can be funny. But the definitive treatment was left to that most awkward of "comedies", *Troilus and Cressida*. Its postponement there, all questions of Shakespeare's inner development excluded, brings with it certain advantages. Chivalry does belong, formally, to the history plays. It is a vestigial residue of past thinking, a fossil perhaps, but still geologically apt. In a play about the Trojan War, strained as the events are through the mediaeval treatments, the chivalric elements have coalesced into a formal anachronism.

II

Chivalry is a dimension of *Troilus and Cressida,* in which the play constantly presents itself. It is not a stratum, not a sub-plot, but a recurring allusion to the world of Malory and Froissart. All the main actors acknowledge as an ideal of conduct this mode of being. One must emphasize this, for commentators have gone too far in stressing the differences between Greeks and Trojans.[8] Directors must do what they can to separate visually the warring camps, and to bring out separate generic characteristics, of which the text supplies hints. But in truth the Greeks and Trojans are not ideologically opposed. Both sides fight for honour, for prestige, for sheer stubbornness and necessity: they have a similarity of outlook and values. They mingle easily enough at the truce, and have a shared past. The "Greekish embassy", which Hector recalls to Ulysses, is a reminder of the diplomatic exchanges which aristocrats in all eras have been accustomed to make. Chivalry unites Greeks and Trojans – even if the plot requires that one side own to chivalry's black sheep, Achilles. In pursuing the mode in *Troilus and Cressida* one needs to track two sorts of word: the object, which is basically a stage prop, and the idea. The ideas animate the objects.

Prologue, first. Its general retreat from confident assertiveness is marked. That fractional hesitation which both reader and audience experience after "A prologue arm'd, but not in confidence", before the next line picks up with "Of author's pen or actor's voice" is the clue to the whole. For our purposes here, the interesting word is *pavilion*. That is a word which any stage designer has to pause over. The *OED* gives "A tent: chiefly applied to one of a large or stately kind, rising to a peak above." Its associations are glamorous and chivalric; in Shakespeare it is the dwelling of Cleopatra, of Henry V, of the Princess of France. But after Prologue's "brave pavilions" (l. 15), the word occurs only once more in *Troilus and Cressida*. It is replaced by the far homelier *tent* ("a portable shelter"), which in singular and plural forms is mentioned 32 times. It is like *Henry V*: Chorus is the official spokesman for the invasion, the play shows us the real thing; Prologue here sees *pavilions,* the play shows *tents*.

Troilus, in his opening scenes, is evidently a Petrarchan. His character-note trope is, for 1602, distinctly passé:

> Why should I war without the walls of Troy,
> That find such cruel battle here within?
>
> (I. i. 2–3)

A little later he speaks, unbelievably, of her hand "In whose comparison all whites are ink" (58), after which a reasonably sophisticated playgoer of 1602 – whether or not an Inns of Court man – might find it hard to take Troilus seriously. If we accept the usual mid-nineties dating of the Sonnets, Shakespeare was savaging this kind of language – see Sonnet 130 – some seven years earlier. Troilus is placed, beyond doubt, when he passes across the stage in an emblem scene. Pandarus (presumably on the upper stage, with Cressida) cries "Brave Troilus! The prince of chivalry!" (I. ii. 230–1) Chivalry is devalued in advance through Pandarus's tone, and the knowing sexuality of the preceding conversation. Cressida is no ingénue, and Troilus by implication emerges as a young fool. This amour scarcely illustrates a troubadour's song. Chivalry, if it has to rest on the sloping shoulders of Troilus, looks to be in poor shape.

The Council scene of Act I, scene iii, obviously a corrosive analysis of the Greek war effort, continues the subversive drift. We can pick it up at the neat caricature of chivalry in Thersites' version of Nestor "Arming to answer in a night alarm" (171), after which a key word is introduced to signal a counter-movement.

Agamemnon   What trumpet? Look, Menelaus.

(213)

Aeneas now enters, with language that is not subverted:

> May one that is a herald and a prince
> Do a fair message to his kingly eye?
>
> (218–19)

Shakespeare does nothing to undermine Aeneas, with his poise, courtesy, and breeding.[9] The officers of heraldry and chivalry are spotless. One needs this (bearing in mind Montjoy) to set against the notion that *Troilus and Cressida* is a one-note lampoon of chivalry. Aeneas's instrument and extension is the *trumpet:* "I bring a trumpet to awake his ear" (251), an association repeated at 256 and 263. *Trumpet* occurs 15 times in *Troilus and Cressida*, more than twice any other play in the canon. (*King Lear* has six, all to do with the Act v combat.) The associations of *trumpet* are invariably with kingly power *(Hamlet)*, with heraldry *(Richard II)*, or as here with parley between opposing forces. It is the ritualized language of truce and parley, a mode of communication signifying equality of speaker and hearer, and acquiescence in common values. When Aeneas gives the command, the trumpeter breaks in upon a sterile debate with a genuine challenge. Here – as with the *alarums* and *drum* that punctuate the military scenes in *Coriolanus* – we discern the hand of Shakespeare the director. The sound of "the silver, snarling trumpets" is the background music to *Troilus and Cressida*.

After this prelude, the challenge which Aeneas delivers from Hector to the Greeks is the essence of chivalry:

> If there be one among the fair'st of Greece
> That holds his honour higher than his ease
> And feeds his praise more than he fears his peril,
> That knows his valour, and knows not his fear,
> That loves his mistress more than in confession
> With truant vows to her own lips he loves,
> And dare avow her beauty and her worth
> In other arms than hers – to him this challenge.
> Hector, in view of Troyans and of Greeks,
> Shall make it good, or do his best to do it,
> He hath a lady, wiser, fairer, truer,

> Than ever Greek did couple in his arms,
> And will tomorrow with his trumpet call
> Midway between your tents and walls of Troy,
> To rouse a Grecian that is true in love.
> If any come, Hector shall honour him;
> If none, he'll say in Troy when he retires,
> The Grecian dames are sunburnt and not worth
> The splinter of a lance.
>
> (I. iii. 265–83)

More than a series of glowing abstractions ("honour", "valour", "beauty"), an imperishable model of conduct is presented. There is the knight, ready to do battle with like-minded idealists in the name of his mistress. (What mistress, one asks? Surely not the put-upon Andromache?) The stereotype of chivalry is complete in every detail, and Nestor, repository of the Greek folk memory, has no doubt that Aeneas must be answered in kind. It is open to the audience to take

> I'll hide my silver beard in a gold beaver,
> And in my vantbrace put my withered brawns,
> And meeting him will tell him that my lady
> Was fairer than his grandam, and as chaste
> As may be in the world.
>
> (296–300)

as pure caricature, one moreover dependent upon its not being taken seriously, or as a rueful acknowledgement that the challenge is real and calls for a response in kind from worthier antagonists. Agamemnon, rising to the occasion, meets the Trojan tone:

> Fair Lord Aeneas, let me touch your hand;
> To our *pavilion* shall I lead you, sir.
> Achilles shall have word of this intent;
> So shall each lord of Greece, from tent to tent.
> Yourself shall feast with us, before you go,
> And find the welcome of a noble foe.
>
> (304–9)

It is interesting to note how Agamemnon, after two lines of blank verse, finds that "intent" leads him involuntarily into "tent"; he is drawn into a rhyme scheme, and a jogging couplet fixes his exit. It is a subtle declension of form. *Pavilion* (I assume there is only one in the Greek camp: Agamemnon has it) yields to *tent*, and the reference stays there. *Pavilion* is nowhere repeated. It is used here to underline the courtesy of Agamemnon's response, and his insistence on a code of shared values.

But the play remorselessly eats away at its own proposed values. The pretence that Hector's challenge is a defence of womanhood is continued into the Trojan debate of Act II, scene ii, in which the entire war is justified as a defence of Helen:

> *Troilus*   She is a theme of honour and renown,
> A spur to valiant and magnanimous deeds,
> Whose present courage may beat down our foes,
> And fame in time to come canonize us;
>
> (II. ii. 199–202)

Glory, honour, renown: the word that contains them all is *fame,* which opens *Love's Labour's Lost* and is seen there as subject to Time and Death. *Fame* is a word of great resonance for the Renaissance.[10] Hector gives the game away, with his volte-face in favour of "our joint and several dignities", i.e. prestige. "Dignities" is at least a reality of sorts. Helen as Immaculate Womanhood is an ideal demolished by her corporeal presence. Act III, scene i (the only scene in which Helen appears), with its remorseless café-chatter, is itself a refutation of the Trojan war aims. And, of course, the Greek.

How complete the demolition is appears only in the final lines of III. i, and then by scandalous implication. The scene has been written entirely in prose, perfectly apt for the boulevard-comedy quality of the dialogue. After Pandarus's departure, Paris and Helen are left alone, and the dialogue he initiates is in verse. It is a complete change of tone and mood, signifying (after the company-gaiety of the encounter à trois) a reversion to seriousness:

> *Sound a retreat*

> *Paris*   They're come from the field. Let us to Priam's hall,
> To greet the warriors. Sweet Helen, I must woo you
> To help unarm our Hector. His stubborn buckles,
> With these your white enchanting fingers touch'd,

> Shall more obey than to the edge of steel
> Or force of Greekish sinews. You shall do more
> Than all the island kings – disarm great Hector.

Helen   'Twill make us proud to be his servant, Paris.
> Yea, what he shall receive of us in duty
> Gives us more palm of beauty than we have,
> Yea, overshines itself.

Paris   Sweet, above thought I love you.

> (III . i. 148–59)

The trumpet sounds a further *retreat* from the postures of chivalry.
The erotic import of Paris's suggestion is marked. "Help unarm",
"disarm", is also to undress: "white enchanting fingers touch'd"
conveys an insidious message. Hector is to "obey" – but in what?
The text refuses to go beyond the hint; but the speculation is easy.
The only threat to the Helen–Paris idyll comes from an arranged
return of Helen to the Greeks, and this has been seriously mooted in
the Trojan Council scene. Why should the Trojans fight for one
man's pleasure? Priam himself has said it, "You have the honey
still, but these the gall" (144), and the debate has hinged on
Hector's decision. Helen's favours, shared with Hector, will ensure
his continuing support for the Trojan war effort. Helen, understanding Paris's drift, answers in verse and in kind: *servant, serve* have long
held sexual implications. The main point however is that Helen
acquiesces in Paris's proposal, finding words – "proud", "duty",
"palm in beauty" – that will cover the indicated actions with a
luminous sheen. And Paris, relieved at Helen's instant understanding and assent, hastens to reassure her of his continuing love for her.
Whether the decision is wrenchingly difficult for him, whether he
takes over Pandarus's role with Pandarus's emotions, the text does
not speak to.

III

The central scene (Act III, scene ii) begins the serious examination
of *faith*. Of the 24 references in *Troilus and Cressida*, a handful come
early and are simply exclamations ("i'faith", "faith"). Troilus is the
first to use the word as a substantive, when it takes on the weight of
his relationship with Cressida: "Few words to fair faith" (94), "my
firm faith" (107). Their dialogue is far from a simple, if nervous,

sexual encounter. It is a sustained revelation of doubt and uncertainty on each side: how can they be sure? *Faith* is Troilus's pledge, the word that knits them together and that registers their severance:

> The fractions of her *faith* . . .
> Of her o'ereaten *faith*, are given to Diomed.
> (v. ii. 162–4)

Equally, it is the word that marks the code of honour to which Hector subscribes and that binds him to the Greeks:

> *Hector* And I do stand engag'd to many Greeks,
> Even in the *faith* of valour, to appear
> This morning to them . . .
> I must not break my *faith*.
> (v. iii. 68–71)

The linking of the two major actions, in *faith*, places the word at the play's centre. One faith is kept, one broken; both pledgers are lost.

Again, the recoil after assertion: Act IV, scene i, brings together second-rate Greek and second-rate Trojan. The initial tone is set by Aeneas, whose debonair welcome of Diomedes as a worthy foe registers the chivalric ideal:

> Health to you, valiant sir,
> During all question of the gentle truce
> . . . In humane gentleness,
> Welcome to Troy!
> (IV. i. 12–13, 22–3)

Diomedes, in professing "mine emulous honour" (30) is not far behind. Paris's summary-comment is like the early oxymora out of *Romeo and Juliet:*

> This is the most despiteful gentle greeting,
> The noblest hateful love, that e'er I heard of
> (34–5)

The encounter is indeed a dramatized oxymoron. But it needs Aeneas to maintain the tone at that level. He exits, and the other two are left alone. Shakespeare has an acute sense of a primal social fact, that there is all the difference in the world between a conversation of three (or more) and two. The discourse of Paris and Diomedes has a brutal, intimate accuracy that is disturbing even in this play. Paris, taken in by the apparent bonhomie of the occasion, asks a question that succeeds in being at once silly, vulgar, and offensive:

> And tell me, noble Diomed, faith tell me true,
> Even in the soul of sound good-fellowship,
> Who, in your thoughts, deserves fair Helen best,
> Myself or Menelaus?
>
> (53–6)

Which merits and receives the iron rigour of Diomedes' response:

> Both alike.
> He merits well to have her that doth seek her,
> Not making any scruple of her soilure,
> With such a hell of pain and world of charge
> (56–9)

His concluding rhymed couplet has a coarse power all the more jarring for its linguistic flatness:

> Both merits pois'd, each weighs nor less nor more;
> But he as he, the heavier for a whore.
>
> (67–8)

Diomedes, much more than Thersites, has claims to be the play's spokesman. The "hell of pain and world of charge" he perceives as the cost of this war for Helen is no other than the truth. Paris, shaken, has no real answer. In this scene, *Troilus and Cressida* closes into its true mode, posturing rebuked by reality.

The play now moves into the symbolic dawning of day, and this is the stage horizon for Troilus's departure in Act IV, scene ii. Shakespeare writes in a bleakly good-humoured sketch of the end to an amour, the young man stealing away at daylight and solicitous, when halted, for his lover's health ("The morn is cold"). When the bad news comes, Troilus's instinct is not to storm, but to ask "Is it so concluded?" and a moment later he is not too overcome to murmur "And, my Lord Aeneas, / We met by chance; you did not find me here" (72–3). This is admirable self-possession, in one who is Ruined; but the sums don't add up. (This might also be the place to mention the one great topic that is never, by word or implication, touched on by Troilus and Cressida: marriage.) Troilus, instead of petitioning Priam, is content with the role of Bereft Lover in IV. iv. It is a self-casting. Chivalry has now emerged as mere posturing, and this is formalized into the parting. Troilus stiffens into "I speak not 'be thou true' as fearing thee, / For I will throw my *glove* to Death himself / That there's no maculation in thy heart" (62–4). The props of the affair become *glove* (Cressida's) and *sleeve* (Troilus's), objects which illustrate symbolically the transactions of Act V. They are subsumed in the glowing couplet with which Aeneas ends the scene:

> The glory of our Troy doth this day lie
> On his *fair* worth and single *chivalry*.
> (IV. iv. 147–8)

Next comes the truce and combat scene of Act IV, scene v. The chivalric pretensions are now too openly discredited to be anything but an invitation to stage business,[11] and the by-play with *trumpet* provides some sour notes. Ajax's command to his trumpeter has to be read twice to be disbelieved:

> Now crack thy lungs, and split thy brazen pipe.
> Blow, villain, till thy sphered bias cheek
> Outswell the colic of puff'd Aquilon.
> Come, stretch thy chest, and let thy eyes spout blood;
> Thou blowest for Hector.
> (IV. v. 7–11)

"No trumpet answers" is the stage direction, voiced by Ulysses, and silence is the best comment on Ajax's rhetoric. Then follows Cressida's entrance. Again, for all the lumpish gestures of gallantry made by the Greeks, this is a cartoon of chivalry, Hanoverians viewed by Gillray. Cressida is kissed by the top five on the Greek General Staff before Diomedes tactfully interposes, and bears her off. The combination of lip-smacking and Ulysses' needling of Cressida is peculiarly unpleasant; no wonder Cressida calls Diomedes "my sweet guardian" (v. ii. 8). And that is chivalry when it, more or less, is working.

Chivalry appears in better shape for the combat, with its preliminaries and aftermath. Greeks and Trojans rise to a self-conscious level of chivalric emulation: the word *knight* (used six times in the scene) helps define the event. Aeneas, the herald/presenter, describes the combatants admiringly to Achilles (77–86), and makes it plain that this is to be no killing-match. Achilles takes the point: "A maiden battle, then?" and the event is signalled as an exhibition bout. (We can note that the "lance" of Hector's challenge has been quietly dropped: were lances too dangerous?) This is to be a best-behaviour scene for all. Diomedes becomes "Sir Diomed", a "gentle knight" (88) – this is undiluted *Faerie Queene* – and Troilus is a "true knight" (96), admiringly characterized by Aeneas to Ulysses and faithfully reported by Ulysses to Agamemnon. Unlike the Romans in *Julius Caesar,* the Trojans and Greeks become *not* ultra-Trojan/Greek (the national is not a dimension of being in *Troilus and Cressida*) but ultra-chivalric, cosmopolitan, citizens of the world. This is the mode that governs them, and Agamemnon sums it all up in his great speech that ends

> But in this extant moment, *faith* and *troth,*
> Strain'd purely from all hollow bias-drawing,
> Bids thee, with most divine integrity,
> From heart of very heart, great Hector, welcome.
>
> (168–71)

That speech, I think, escapes irony: it understands itself: it offers a preservative against Time. So, with exchange of compliments (Ulysses' "Most gentle and most valiant Hector, welcome", 227), the scene is played out, only Achilles being guilty of ungentlemanly conduct. The others are clearly bent on throwing a mutual admiration party.

IV

Of the twin Q.E.D.'s of the play, the first is presented in the discovery scene of Act v, scene ii. *Pledge, sleeve, glove* are the counters with which Shakespeare demonstrates his moves: it is diagrammatic, an affair of blackboards. Troilus is left with a theorem he cannot master, "to square the general sex / By Cressid's rule" (135–6), and a personal débâcle he can neither understand nor resolve. It is left to Ulysses to take over the play's voice and speak with compassion and courtesy: "What hath she done, Prince, that can soil our mothers?" (137) Even Troilus can discipline himself to "My courteous lord, adieu . . . Accept distracted thanks" (189, 193). The code, even in defeat, has something to be said for it.

And this is true of the final battle's outcome. It is mounted in the terms we have come to recognize: "I am today i'th'vein of chivalry" says Hector (v. iii. 32). Sparing captive Greeks is "fair play" (43), close enough to modern usage. Time and again this play, with fey anticipation, hints at the language and attitudes of the English public school 300 years on, at the most mannered attributes of Georgian poetry. It is as though the play understands that anachronisms of thought are destined to repeat themselves in giant cycles of history, will return in waves spanning centuries. "I must not break my faith" (71) is Hector's motto-statement, and the basis of his tragedy. The actual battle-scenes unleash a flood of wild, anarchic glee in the audience. "Now the sleeve, now the sleeve!" (v. iv. 25) reduces the event to a spectator sport, Thersites representing the less seemly sort of onlooker. In the encounter between Thersites and the cream of chivalry, Hector displays a divine fatuousness: "Art thou of blood and honour?" (v. iv. 27) Is he parodying himself, or is this the standard Shakespearean intensification of mode which his actors must work with? The latter, I think. The best contingent evidence is Diomedes', as he opens the scene that follows:

> Go, go, my servant, take thou Troilus' horse;
> Present the fair steed to my lady Cressid.
> Fellow, commend my service to her beauty;
> Tell her I have chastis'd the amorous Troyan,
> And am her knight by proof.
>
> (v. v. 1–5)

Better dialogue has been written in movie epics of the 1950s. It is pure Wardour Street, every line. Note the vocative possessive of "my servant" (cf. "my liege", "my queen") – even the servant has a role in Diomedes' costume–drama – and the decadent Romanticism of "steed", "chastis'd", "amorous Troyan". We are long past the days when disintegrationists could view such tosh as evidence that Shakespeare did not write the passage. It is on the contrary the strongest proof that he did: Shakespeare is using language of terminal mediocrity to place the speaker. There is a complete world of imaginative self-identification in Diomedes' five lines. You could place them underneath a painting by someone on the Pre-Raphaelite fringe, pass the whole off as early Rossetti, and hope to get away with it.

The first five lines of Act v, scene v are Diomedes' version of the chivalric ideal. Chivalry appears in better shape with Hector, as his "Pause, if thou wilt" indicates in conjunction with Achilles' "I do disdain thy courtesy, proud Troyan" (v. vi. 14–15). This shows well, the sparing of an out-of-condition opponent. Yet Hector ends the scene in pursuit of a retreating foe who wants only to live. The *appetite* that Nestor detects in Hector (v. v. 27) – it is the same foe that Ulysses names in his great speech – is explicitly presented: Hector is not above killing a man for his armour. This "goodly armour" is the final symbol of chivalry, and "Most putrefied core, so fair without" (v. viii. 1) its own epitaph. Hector's vain "I am unarm'd. Forgo this vantage, Greek" is a final flicker of the chivalric spirit, meeting no more response than Ajax's trumpeter: "No trumpet sounds." What Hector actually encounters is a rhyme – this play so often expresses itself in the flat assertiveness of rhyme – Achilles' "Strike, fellows, strike! This is the man I seek." Achilles' rhyme rebuts Hector's proposition. And the Greek's dreadful final couplet is the logical (cheval) reduction of chivalry:

> Come, tie his body to my horse's tail;
> Along the field I will the Trojan trail.
> (v. viii. 21–2)

Is this the play's last word on the chivalric spirit? No. The triumph of satire is not an unconditional surrender of the opposing forces, and the defeat of chivalry is tinged with pity and regret. Here as always, the countervailing spirit of Shakespeare lodges reservations against the play's own apparent propositions. Aeneas, the great founder of Rome, is left unrefuted; not for him to *Sound a retreat.* "Stand, ho! Yet are we masters of the field. / Never go home; here starve we out the night" (v. x. 1–2). There's cool resolution there, no bragging or inner collapse. Aeneas has the right to rebuke Troilus, "My lord, you do discomfort all the host." The play has nothing further to allege against Cressida (who has entered the final plea in her own defence), and she remains unpilloried. She has, after all, secured the best available terms for herself as the only woman in a military camp. Ajax leaves the idea of decency intact, with "Great Hector was as good a man as he" (v. ix. 6). And Agamemnon, courteous and magnanimous, declines to crow:

> March patiently along. Let one be sent
> To pray Achilles see us in our tent.
> If in his death the gods have us befriended,
> Great Troy is ours, and our sharp wars are ended.
>
> (v. ix. 7–10)

The mood of exhaustion that suffuses the close contains a weary gratitude that it is all over now, or will be soon. Achilles' report to his commanding officer will not be mentioned in dispatches, but it brings the end of the war in sight. Troilus and Pandarus share the unpleasantness of the last words, but the final stages have left chivalry alive. The play merely states that it hasn't worked, this time.

9   The Masque of *Henry VIII*

Of all Shakespeare's plays, *Henry VIII* is the most resistant to change on the stage. The record of performance shows variation rather than a shift of perception: we learn that Irving's Lyceum production was popular but ruinously expensive, that Beerbohm Tree spread the spectacle over four hours, that Tyrone Guthrie speeded matters up somewhat; it is the same object, always.[1] The recent television production (Kevin Billington's, for BBC TV, 1979) offers the illusion of intimacy, but in fact approaches the characters no more closely than could the past. The play is for general purposes a costume spectacular. As such, its infrequent revivals work perfectly well; and J. C. Trewin, noting that "Because 1953 was Coronation year, the Vic did *Henry VIII*, an almost regulation choice"[2] makes in effect a general comment on the play's essence. And yet there is something in *Henry VIII* that is at odds with a modern revival. Peter Hall is quoted as saying to Kevin Billington, "I hear you're doing *Henry VIII;* I managed to avoid that for twenty [*sic*] years at the RSC."[3] The usual glosses – that *Henry VIII* is second rate, that there is a genuine authorship problem – by-pass the issue. It is better to point out that the close, unillusioned analysis of politics, which the RSC had conducted so successfully in *The Wars of the Roses* and the subsequent histories, altogether fails to work with *Henry VIII*. The play repels close analysis. It repels irony, it repels ambiguity, it repels scrutiny. If there is one history play in the canon that pays no dues to Brecht, it is *Henry VIII*.

The substantive reason is clear enough. *Henry VIII* honours a defunct form, the masque. At once, this concept offers a description of the play, albeit critical: "To account for the play as an imitation of the masque is to emphasize what most of us find disappointing in it: its lack of sensitivity to political ambiguity, its shallow characterization, its facile religious orthodoxy."[4] Agreed, this would be an inadequate description; and "A better answer . . . is that Shakespeare followed contemporary fashion in his last play by adapting it to the spirit and principles of the court masque."[5] That

128

is the right line of approach, for *Henry VIII* cannot be assessed in negatives. It is a dramatic experiment which incorporates a deal of masque-like spectacle, and goes much further in taking over the assumptions of the masque. I want to show how the assumptions of the masque govern the consciousness of the audience.

I

The prologue offers an immediate statement of the play's decorum. It is a class affair. "I come no more to make you laugh" (l. 1) is a hint that plebeian coarseness is out of place here, a hint developed into "Only they / That come to hear a merry bawdy play, / A noise of targets, or to see a fellow / In a long motley coat guarded with yellow, / Will be deceiv'd" (13–17). The note is one of exclusivity, confirmed by the reference to the "shilling" entrance money, a sum well beyond most pockets. The audience, "The first and happiest hearers of the town" (24) is to mark "Such noble scenes as draw the eye to flow" (4), and the key term (to which I shall return) is *noble*. The attitude inculcated by the prologue is one of decorous pity, and the social assurance to the "*gentle* hearers" (17) is stressed throughout: this play is for gentry, who will know how to behave.

Show or tell is the playwright's eternal choice. *Henry VIII,* so often concerned with showing, offers in the first scene the telling of a great event. The Field of the Cloth of Gold is

> The view of earthly glory. Men might say
> Till this time pomp was single, but now married
> To one above itself. Each following day
> Became the next day's master, till the last
> Made former wonders its. Today the French,
> All clinquant, all in gold, like heathen gods,
> Shone down the English; and, tomorrow, they
> Made Britain India – every man that stood
> Show'd like a mine. Their dwarfish pages were
> As cherubins, all gilt. The madams too,
> Not us'd to toil, did almost sweat to bear
> The pride upon them, that their very labour
> Was to them as a painting. Now this masque
> Was cried incomparable:
>
> (I. i. 14–27)

The event itself becomes a *masque:* Norfolk's speech leaves the term undefined, for it may refer to a formal entertainment (which the description much resembles) or assert the encounter itself to be an episode of political theatre. That ambiguity is central to the play. What matters is not only the event, but the attitudes to the event that the play enjoins. They are wholly admiring. There is no reservation permitted to Norfolk's total admiration, and Buckingham's keen regret that illness kept him away. The point here is sustained by history, that those entitled to attend a great diplomatic function must do so, unless for sound medical reasons. Behind what might seem pure sycophancy, or naive acquiescence in a great show, is an ideology. It emerges in Norfolk's "All was royal; / To the disposing of it nought *rebell'd,* / Order gave each thing view" (I. i. 42–4). The values of political loyalty are assimilated into the decorum of performance and response. That is the true function of the masque.

The same conditioning is promoted more subtly in Act I, scene iv, whose ceremonial aspects are signalled by the initial stage direction:

Hautboys. A small table under a state for the Cardinal, *a longer table for the guests. Then enter* Anne Bullen *and divers other Ladies and Gentlemen as guests, at one door; at another door, enter* Sir Henry Guildford.

But this is not a great State banquet. More enticingly, it is an intimate dinner party, where the King might – just – drop in. The conversation is not of politics, but the preliminaries to a sexual skirmish:

Chamberlain	Sweet ladies, will it please you sit? Sir Harry,
	Place you that side; I'll take charge of this.
	His Grace is ent'ring. Nay, you must not freeze;
	Two women plac'd together makes cold weather.
	My Lord Sands, you are one will kept 'em waking;
	Pray, sit between these ladies.
Sands	By my faith,
	And thank your lordship. By your leave, sweet ladies.
	If I chance to talk a little wild, forgive me;
	I had it from my father.
Anne	Was he mad, sir?
Sands	O, very mad, exceeding mad, in love too.
	But he would bite none; just as I do now,

	He would kiss you twenty with a breath.
Chamberlain	Well said, my lord.
	So, now y'are fairly seated. Gentlemen,
	The penance lies on you, if these fair ladies
	Pass away frowning.
Sands	For my little cure,
	Let me alone.

(19–35)

The social badinage is admirably done, and the shading of protocol with sexual opportunity knowingly presented. To be present at such a gathering is less a by-product than a central reward for participating in the process of State. And then, after Wolsey's welcome to his guests, the scene becomes overtly a "masque scene", since Henry and his followers enter *as masquers, habited like shepherds, usher'd by the Lord Chamberlain.* A dance follows.[6] This scene is an image of courtly revelry, whose leitmotiv is *noble:* "this noble bevy" (4), "this fair company" (7), "That noble lady / Or gentleman" (36–7), "a noble troop of strangers" (54), "Go, give 'em welcome; you can speak the French tongue; / And pray receive 'em nobly" (58–9), "A noble company!" (68). The Concordance confirms the impression of designed repetition, for *noble* occurs 47 times in *Henry VIII,* more than in any other play in the canon save *Coriolanus* (58). *Noble* is not a term confined to the narrowest definition of class. The values of *nobility* embrace all present, who include commoners (Sir Henry Guildford, Sir Thomas Lovell, and others) and the King himself (referred to in a later scene as "a most noble judge, the King my master", v. iii. 101). The effect is a glamorous and glittering picture of the nobility at its revels in, as it were, semi-private intimacy. Van Dyck, the great master of courtly imagery, perfected 20 years later the impressions that Fletcher and Shakespeare sketched here. The theatre audience is flattered by being made privy to a noble occasion. *We* join the nobility: that is the subliminal assurance. To appreciate the revels of Act I, scene iv places us in a small and discerning group, the socially elect.

II

The revels, like all else in this play, have as their focal point the King. Without the King there is nothing. The earlier histories show us a people with independent existence. The England of *Henry IV* needs good government but will survive anyway. Without the monarch, all in *Henry VIII* goes wrong, or cannot function: the adjustments, the corrections, the decisions of the King are presented as vital to the proper functioning of the body politic. It is of course a homage to the tidal doctrine of the seventeenth century, the infallibility and all-supremacy of the monarch. All the main actors in *Henry VIII* display (within their limits) an exemplary submissiveness to the King's will. Abergavenny's "The will of heaven be done, and the King's pleasure / By me obey'd (I. i. 215–16) states it most clearly, and he echoes his leader, Buckingham, who a moment before had identified the King's will with the will of heaven. At no point do the actors challenge the authority and wisdom of the King. Rebellion is inconceivable: worse than a crime, a solecism.

But what is the nature of this centre of authority and wisdom? The play does not precisely draw back from examining Authority. Rather, it states that Authority is of its nature public and gestural. The old distinction between the public and private man is abandoned, and the King emerges as a totally public being. The touches of pseudo-intimacy which Henry shares with other dramatis personae make only the most limited of physical statements. The King, when he broaches the matter of his marriage "did reek" (II. iv. 206). This sounds interesting, until one remembers that the French madams "did almost sweat" in their Court finery (I. i. 24), and that Buckingham "sweat extremely" at his trial (II. i. 33). It is a mere trick, a journalist's device to manufacture immediacy. The essential truth is that the King is the main actor in the drama of State.

> *King*   Arise, and take place by me. Half your suit
> Never name to us; you have half our power.
> The other moi'ty, ere you ask, is given;
> Repeat your will and take it.
>
>   (I. ii. 10–13)

It is useless to point out that these words are not true, that Henry is bent on depriving his wife of her title. Such thoughts rise easily, and the play as easily suppresses them. The play affirms: the words *are* true, and Henry is illustrating a model of imperial courtesy and respect for due form. Henry, in respecting the protocol of royal conduct, teaches a lesson in social conduct to his entire realm. This scene, like all the other scenes in which Henry figures, indicates that he is not to be judged by the same standards of psychological intimacy as the rulers in the previous histories. That would be indecorous, a violation of the masque's convention. Put more simply: Henry has no soliloquy. How could he? What could he say to himself? And how can this play admit that he has a private self to be addressed?

Henry's mode favours the static, the typical. On Wolsey's defence, he comments:

> Fairly answer'd!
> A loyal and obedient subject is
> Therein *illustrated*
> (III. ii. 179–81)

as though the function of political episodes and actors were to adorn in visual form a book of exemplary maxims. Interestingly, Wolsey had seemed earlier to propose a dynamic of state opposed to so static a view:

> We must not stint
> Our necessary actions in the fear
> To cope malicious censurers, which ever,
> As rav'nous fishes, do a vessel follow
> That is new-trimmed, but benefit no further
> Than vainly longing. What we oft do best,
> By sick interpreters, once weak ones, is
> Not ours, or not allow'd; what worst, as oft,
> Hitting a grosser quality, is cried up
> For our best act. If we shall stand still,
> In fear our motion will be mock'd or carp'd at,
> We should take root here where we sit, or sit
> State-statues only.
> (I. ii. 76–88)

"State-statues only" is the true challenge to the King, and not the manifest issue of a one-sixth capital levy. In Wolsey's dynamic of action, rulers must be prepared to back policy with unpopular acts – such as raising taxes. Monarchs know well the permanent virtues of popularity. They also know the advantages of having unpopular ministers, whom they can check or dismiss. Henry opts for the roles of Guardian of Precedent, Defender of the Law, and Scourge of

Bureaucratic Abuse. This looks better than being a *State-statue only;* but it comes to much the same thing.

It is an assumption of the masque that role governs behaviour. The human touches which the dramatis personae display *in extremis* are checked by their own self-discipline and sense of the role's decorum. Buckingham, on receiving his judgment

> was stirr'd
> With such an agony he sweat extremely,
> And something spoke in choler, ill and hasty.
> But he fell to himself again, and sweetly
> In all the rest show'd a most *noble* patience.
>
> (II. i. 32–6)

His dignified final speech acknowledges the decorum of state: "I had my trial, / And must needs say, a *noble* one; which makes me / A little happier than my wretched father" (II. i. 118–20). A noble trial is some kind of spiritual solace. Buckingham has starred in a major scene of state. But the tendency of *Henry VIII* is to turn individuals into types, or roles. Katherine sees herself as "a wife, a true one" (III. i. 126), "A woman . . . Never yet branded with suspicion" (127–8), "a constant woman to her husband" (133). Above all:

> *Queen Katherine*   My lord, I dare not make myself so guilty
> To give up willingly that *noble title*
> Your master wed me to.
>
> (139–41)

It confirms Henry's own praise of her, "She's *noble* born; / And like her true *nobility* she has carried herself towards me" (II. iv. 139–41). Even her deathbed scene is emblematic:

> *Queen Katherine*   Let me be us'd with honour. Strew me over
> With maiden flowers, that all the world may know
> I was a chaste wife to my grave. Embalm me,
> Then lay me forth. Although unqueen'd, yet like
> A queen, and daughter to a king, inter me.
>
> (IV. ii. 167–72)

In *Henry VIII*, "noble title" is the role above all others. It is the existential state of the players. "I am Duchess of Malfi still" could be echoed by all the major characters. No one steps out of his part, no one contests the role.

III

And where does this leave irony, the constant presence of the earlier histories? Irony is all but suppressed. Very occasionally, one catches a glint in the playwright's eye. *Suffolk:* "No, his conscience / Has crept too near another lady" (II. ii. 17–18). *Wolsey:* "The King has cur'd me, / I humbly thank his Grace" (III. ii. 380–1). Such rare hints are never developed. Cromwell's reactions to Wolsey's fall rebut irony.

> O my lord,
> Must I, then, leave you? Must I needs forgo
> So good, so noble, and so true a master?
> Bear witness, all that have not hearts of iron,
> With what sorrow Cromwell leaves his lord.
> The King shall have my service, but my pray'rs
> For ever and for ever shall be yours.
>
> (III. ii. 422–7)

And:

> *Wolsey*   Cromwell, I charge thee, fling away ambition!
> By that sin fell the angels.
>
> (III. ii. 440–1)

And yet the audience knows who Cromwell is.

Clearly, the drama cannot be monolithic in its domination of the audience's thought-processes. There is a mild challenge to the oppressive decorum of the piece in Act V, scene i, when the Old Lady wants more than a hundred marks for saying that the baby is just like Henry. This softens and humanizes the play's tendencies. (It is worth noting that Tyrone Guthrie chose to have the Prologue spoken by the Old Lady; the obvious choice would have been one of the choric Gentlemen.[7]) Such moments are mitigation, not denial. This play is not so much guilty of self-lobotomy, as exercising its intelligence to suppress much of what is knows. *Henry VIII*, like so many of its characters, stands on disciplined guard over its own knowledge.

Of what, then, does the knowledge, or consciousness of *Henry VIII* consist? Its consciousness is that of Chorus, whose expression here is assigned to a number of speakers. Chorus in this play is an affair of gentry. Griffith, for example, "an honest chronicler" (IV. ii. 72), instructs Katherine and the audience how to assess her late adversary. It is a lesson in magnanimity. Chorus functions as "herald" (69) there; the discreet exchanges of Act II, scene i are closer to the nerve-ends of this play.

> First Gentleman   What may it be? [*pause*] You do not doubt my
> faith, sir?
>   . . . Let me have it;
> I do not talk much.
> . . . We are too open here to argue this;
> Let's think in private more.
>
> (II. i. 142–4, 167–8)

Whatever the glories of living in the reign of Bluff King Hal, these Gentlemen are circumspect enough in their talk – and, more to the point, circumspect about their reasons for circumspection.

It is in IV. i, however, that Chorus reaches its apotheosis. So does the play. I quote in full the extraordinary stage direction:

THE ORDER OF THE CORONATION.

1   *A liuely Flourish of Trumpets.*
2   *Then, two Judges.*
3   *Lord* Chancellor, *with Purse and Mace before him.*
4   Quirristers *singing.*   Musicke.
5   Mayor of London, *bearing the Mace. Then* Garter *in his Coate of Armes, and on his head he wore a Gilt Copper Crowne.*
6   Marquesse Dorset, *bearing a Scepter of Gold, on his head, a Demy Coronall of Gold. With him, the Earle of* Surrey, *bearing the Rod of Silver with the Dove, Crowned with an Earles Coronet. Collars of Esses.*
7   Duke of Suffolke, *in his Robe of Estate, his Coronet on his head bearing a long white Wand, as High Steward. With him, the Duke of* Norfolke, *with the Rod of Marshalship, a Coronet on his head. Collars of Esses.*
8   *A* Canopy, *borne by foure of the* Cinque-Ports, *under it the Queene*

in her Robe, in her haire, richly adorned with Pearle Crowned. On each side her, the Bishops of London, *and* Winchester.

9   *The* Olde Dutchesse of Norfolke, *in a Coronall of Gold, wrought with Flowers bearing the Queenes Traine.*

10   *Certaine* Ladies *or* Countesses, *with plaine Circlets of Gold, without Flowers.*

Exeunt, *first passing over the Stage in Order and State, and then, A great Flourish of Trumpets.*

No wonder that Sir Henry Wootton, in his letter discussing the play, refers to it as *All is True.* That title (or subtitle) is a neat emblem for the play's genre, as it must seem in Act IV, scene i. Let us call it drama-documentary. It is reportage, with a deft blurring of fiction and actuality. Wootton's account catches nicely his ambivalence, a patronizing respect for the players:

> The King's players had a new play, called *All is True,* representing some principal pieces of the reign of Henry VIII, which was set forth with many extraordinary circumstances of pomp and majesty, even to the matting of the stage; the Knights of the Order with their Georges and garters, the Guards with their embroidered coats, and the like: sufficient in truth within a while to make greatness very familiar, if not ridiculous.[8]

That is the deposition of an authentic First Gentleman. He has seen the real thing, and wants his reader to know that the players got it wrong, but made a passable shot at the procession just the same. Now consider the play's commentary on the procession:

Second Gentleman	A royal train, believe me. These I know.
	Who's that that bears the sceptre?
First Gentleman	Marquess Dorset,
	And that the Earl of Surrey, with the rod.
Second Gentleman	A bold brave gentleman. That should be
	The Duke of Suffolk?
First Gentleman	'Tis the same: High Steward.
Second Gentleman	And that my Lord of Norfolk?
First Gentleman	Yes.
Second Gentleman	[*Looking on the* Queen]
	Heaven bless thee!
	Thou hast the sweetest face I ever look'd on.

> Sir, as I have a soul, she is an angel;
> Our King has all the Indies in his arms,
> And more and richer, when he strains that
> lady.
> I cannot blame his conscience.

First Gentleman   They that bear
> The cloth of honour over her are four barons
> Of the Cinque-ports.

Second Gentleman Those men are happy, and so are all near her.
> I take it, she that carries up the train
> Is that old noble lady, Duchess of Norfolk.

First Gentleman It is; and all the rest are countesses.

                                        (IV. i. 37–52)

It is the quintessence of *Tatlery*.[9] So is the First Gentleman's little joke about the countesses's primary attainment: "These are stars indeed." "And sometimes falling ones." "No more of that!" adjures Second Gentleman. (He can scarcely blame First Gentleman, though. The joke is a tonal echo of his own "I cannot blame his conscience", which is about as far as indiscretion can go in *Henry VIII*.) But the contours are clear enough. Call it gossip-column or eye-witness reportage, Act IV, scene i is "the card or calendar of gentry". The facts of personage, costume, and order are detailed with loving precision to a rapt audience. And Third Gentleman, who has procured by nameless means a ticket to the Abbey (the procession is of course viewed outside) hastens out to spread the word on the events indoors. The key to everything is knowingness, that quality which the play imparts and for which the audience pants. It is best caught in Second Gentleman's lofty "I thank you, sir. Had I not known these customs, / I should have been beholding to your paper" (IV. i. 20–1). What the play permits the audience to know is knowingness. The illusion, not the reality of intimacy, is on offer. The common lament of gossip-columnists is that they know nothing of their great subjects.

                                    IV

The play remains to be ended, and Shakespeare and Fletcher make in the final stages a remarkable concession. They let the people in.[10] The Porter and his man (V. iv) are the first plebeians to be exhibited in Henry VIII; and they are engaged in the strikingly symbolic exercise of keeping the crowd at bay. As Alice S. Venezky comments,

> The final [*sic*] scene . . . presents a novel departure from Shakespeare's method of suggesting offstage crowds by a small group of representative spectators on stage. Instead, cries offstage and the lively action of two actors who try to hold off the invisible horde convey the impression of a vast and unruly throng.[11]

The play sites itself, with unerring judgment, on the social sense of the occasion. The crowd in the palace yard is unruly but good-humoured: this is no storming of the Winter Palace, and the main need, as the Lord Chamberlain perceives, is to create a passage for the ladies.

> *Lord Chamberlain*   Where are these porters,
> These lazy knaves? Y'have made a fine hand, fellows!
> There's a trim rabble let in. Are all these
> Your faithful friends o'th'suburbs? We shall have
> Great store of room, no doubt, left for the ladies,
> When they pass back from the christening . . .
> Go, break among the press, and find a way out
> To let the troop pass fairly, or I'll find
> A Marshalsea shall hold ye play these two months.
>
> (v. iv. 68–73, 83–5)

This is clearly a media event. ("Go, break among the press" has curious resonances.) The Lord Chamberlain's Establishment distaste for the multitude is coupled with a recognition that it has a right to be present, and that the problem is one of crowd control. What neutralizes the mob's dangerousness is the very reason for its assembly, the hailing of the new monarch-in-being. So the Monarch is a symbol of social order and control, beyond the apparent disorderliness of the occasion. The last mob in the canon is tamed by Henry. Substantially, Act v, scene iv (and the play at large) suits the consciousness of the Blackfriars audience, for the view taken of the people is evidently patronizing. But the general line is that in spite of a scolding from the Lord Chamberlain, the common people have a right to participate in a great event.

And this is the open statement of the final scene, v. v. At last the play moves beyond the shows and processions of the great, to which the public has limited or no access. Cranmer's address to the infant Elizabeth, "A pattern to all princess" (22), has a Messianic ring: "She shall be, to the happiness of England, / An aged princess" (56–7). The appeal is to the nation, not a class. It is Henry, the shrewdest politician in the drama, who seizes the occasion to ratify the link between Crown and people. His final speech is addressed to Cranmer, then to the Lord Mayor as representing the commonalty. Henry's last eight lines spell it all out:

> I thank ye all. To you, my good Lord Mayor,
> And you, good brethren, I am much beholding;
> I have receiv'd much honour by your presence,
> And ye shall find me thankful. Lead the way, lords.
> Ye must all see the Queen, and she must thank ye,
> She will be sick else. This day, no man think
> H'as business at his house; for all shall stay.
> This little one shall make it holiday.
>
> (70–7)

After the royal domination of high politics, the play offers an image of royal populism. It is really the application of the lessons that Henry IV inculcated to his son in *1 Henry IV* (III. ii). The people become "good brethren"; largesse will be discreetly dispensed, "And ye shall find me thankful"; the Queen will be on view to the crowds, "She will be sick else"; best of all, the day is to be a public holiday. It would be ungracious to comment that the people present are making it a holiday anyway, with or without Henry's permission. It is the play's purpose to stifle such base observations. In the end, there is no politics like the politics of royalty, when conducted by a master, and Henry understands perfectly that in order to enjoy masques one must cultivate populism. The play thus becomes the tribute of two great professionals, Shakespeare and Fletcher, to another, Henry VIII. It also becomes, as Sir Henry Wootton would insist, journalism.

Something more happens in the last few lines. Henry's speech builds up to that charged word, *holiday*. The people, who have been kept waiting in the wings throughout *Henry VIII*, like the unseen mob of Act v, scene iv, are now to have their reward. At *holiday*, general applause must break out on the stage and in the house, as the masque of populism opens out to the audience. The consciousness of the Blackfriars audience is enlarged into that of the community. The event is however more specifically technical than it looks. What plays well in a private theatre must play in a public one, too. At the last, *Henry VIII* prepares itself for a successful transfer from the Blackfriars to the Globe.

Notes

References are to *The Complete Works of Shakespeare,* ed. David Bevington, 3rd edn (Glenview, Ill.: Scott, Foresman, 1980).

NOTES TO THE INTRODUCTION

1. J. I. M. Stewart, *Character and Motive in Shakespeare* (London: Longmans, 1949) p. 39.
2. Ann Jennalie Cook, *The Privileged Playgoers of Shakespeare's London 1576–1642* (Princeton University Press, 1981).
3. Northrop Frye, *A Natural Perspective: The Development of Shakespearean Comedy and Romance* (New York: Harcourt, Brace & World, 1965) p. viii.

NOTES TO CHAPTER 1: METAMORPHOSES OF THE STAGE

1. It is from Act I, scene ii of *The Roaring Girl,* as quoted by Alfred Harbage in *Shakespeare's Audience* (New York: Columbia University Press, 1961) p. 114. The passage actually describes the elaborately painted walls of a gentleman's parlour, but rests on the theatre analogy. As Harbage says, "A pleasing passage inspired by the audience of the Fortune gives an idea of what Shakespeare saw in the Globe".
2. "The sightlines of the theatre also had an effect upon the acting. Essentially they were poor." See Bernard Beckerman, *Shakespeare at the Globe 1599–1609* (New York: Macmillan, 1962) p. 129.
3. The passage plays on the theatrical and domestic senses of "galleries". Andor Gomme, in his New Mermaid edition of *The Roaring Girl* (London: Ernest Benn, 1976), states that "Sir Alexander's collection suggests a parody of the great collections which began to be made in Elizabeth's reign. . . . Pictures were sometimes fixed to the wall so close together as to make a mosaic covering the wall entirely. The display hints at the spectacular stage effects which were then becoming popular in masques and is a kind of visual diagram of the action of the play" (p. 14). At "floating island", he comments: "A *trompe-l'oeil* effect must be in mind here, intended to draw the audience more completely into the spectacle."
4. I quote from *The Dramatic Works of Thomas Dekker,* ed. Fredson Bowers, 4 vols (Cambridge University Press, 1953–61) II, 584. On it Cyrus Hoy comments: "The appeal for applause at the end of the play is couched in

an image reminiscent of the end of Book ɪ of *The Faerie Queene* (ɪ. xii. 42): 'Now strike your sailes ye iolly Mariners, / For we be come vnto a quiet rode' " (*Introductions, Notes, and Commentaries to Texts in "The Dramatic Works of Thomas Dekker"*, 4 vols (Cambridge University Press, 1980–1) ɪɪ, 383).

5. *The Dramatic Works of Thomas Dekker*, ɪɪ, 393. The final scene in *Westward Ho!* is probably Dekker's.

6. E. K. Chambers, *The Elizabethan Stage*, 4 vols (Oxford: The Clarendon Press, 1923) ɪɪ, 116.

7. Richard Southern, *The Staging of Plays before Shakespeare* (London: Faber, 1973) p. 538.

8. John Cranford Adams, *The Globe Playhouse*, 2nd edn (New York: Barnes & Noble, 1961) p. 304.

9. J. L. Styan, *Shakespeare's Stagecraft* (Cambridge University Press, 1967) p. 19.

10. This is a minority view, but is argued for strongly by Adams, *The Globe Playhouse*, pp. 90–8. If accepted, it makes the platform resemble a crude prow.

11. I use the term that established itself in the later history of the theatre, when the stages sloped down towards the audience.

12. J. L. Styan cites several instances where the text probably indicates a corner of the stage (*Shakespeare's Stagecraft*, p. 18).

13. T. J. B. Spencer, in his New Penguin edition of *Hamlet* (Harmondsworth: Penguin, 1980) p. 254.

14. Cf. the celebrated mime in Peter Shaffer's *The Royal Hunt of the Sun* (National Theatre, 1966), in which the conquistadores climbed the Andes most convincingly – on a level stage.

15. Adams (*The Globe Playhouse*, p. 399) believes that a "mossbank" was used, being "placed in the middle of the Glade, and that on taking his father's hand Edgar helped him to mount". In the most thorough survey of *Lear* staging, Marvin Rosenberg has little to say on the point: "An actual fall from some height has been visualized; but almost certainly Shakespeare intended only the flat stage, to stress·Gloster's illusion. Theatre Edgars have sometimes circled to catch Gloster as he falls, to make clear to audiences that the scenery described in wholly illusory" (*The Masks of King Lear* (Berkeley and Los Angeles: University of California Press, 1972) pp. 264–6).

16. Caroline Spurgeon emphasizes that *The Tempest* is "an absolute symphony of sound", and draws attention to the ever-present sounds of the sea on a small island. See her *Shakespeare's Imagery* (Cambridge University Press, 1935) pp. 300–4.

17. This is not to engage in the controversy over "formal" versus "natural" styles of acting on the Elizabethan stage. A degree of stylization has always been called for in acting. Shakespeare's own colleagues would surely not have ignored the signals built into the text, which presumably reflect the general requirements and practice of the Company.

18. See especially William Strachey's account of the plots and mutinies Sir George had to quell, as printed in *Narrative and Dramatic Sources of Shakespeare*, ed. Geoffrey Bullough, 8 vols (London: Routledge & Kegan Paul, 1957–75) ᴠɪɪɪ, 175–94.

19. The Fortune contract is conveniently reprinted in, for example, Andrew Gurr, *The Shakespearean Stage 1574–1642* (Cambridge University Press, 1970) pp. 92–4, and C. Walter Hodges, *The Globe Restored*, 2nd edn (New York: Norton, 1973) pp. 163–6.

20. A. D. Nuttall, *Two Concepts of Allegory* (London: Routledge & Kegan Paul, 1967) p. 141.

NOTES TO CHAPTER 2: 'RICHARD III': BONDING THE AUDIENCE

1. A. P. Rossiter, *Angel with Horns* (London: Longmans, 1961) p. 2.
2. Nicholas Brooke, *Shakespeare's Early Tragedies* (London: Methuen, 1968) p. 67.
3. Robert Weimann, *Shakespeare and the Popular Tradition in the Theatre: Studies in the Social Dimension of Dramatic Form and Function*, ed. Robert Schwartz (Baltimore, Md: The Johns Hopkins University Press, 1978) p. 68.
4. The practice is codified in Laurence Olivier's film. It is accepted as correct by Brooke, *Shakespeare's Early Tragedies*, p. 56. Bernard Spivack cites an interesting anecdote on this point: it was the experience of Margaret Carrington, who prepared John Barrymore for his Richard III. Barrymore delivered the soliloquy at the end of the Lady Anne wooing scene to himself, with a mediocre response from the audience. Margaret Carrington suggested that he speak directly to the audience; he did, and the reaction was tremendous (*Shakespeare and the Allegory of Evil* (New York: Columbia University Press, 1958) p. 456).
5. Weimann, *Shakespeare and the Popular Tradition*, p. 150. " 'Moralize', in this sense, is a metaphorical statement about the literary history of the verbal figure" (ibid.).
6. Ibid., p. 151.
7. Weimann quotes (ibid., p. 69) a "Tyrant", who introduces himself thus:

> I am full of sotelty,
> ffalshed, gyll, and trechery;
> Therefor am I namyd by clergy
> As mali actoris.

8. Ibid., p. 155.
9. Paul N. Siegel, "Richard III as Businessman", *Shakespeare Jahrbuch* (Weimar), 114 (1978) 106.
10. Wilbur Sanders, in *The Dramatist and the Received Idea* (Cambridge University Press, 1968), gives full weight to the ironic and satiric content of *Richard III*.
11. *King Darius*, printed in 1565: cited by Weimann, *Shakespeare and the Popular Tradition*, p. 111.
12. Weimann, ibid., p. 147.
13. There is also a tradition in the visual arts of such a grouping. The iconography of the king flanked by bishops is discussed by Bridget Gellert Lyons, in "Stage Imagery and Political Symbolism in *Richard III*", *Criticism*, 20 (1978) 21–3.

14. Weimann, *Shakespeare and the Popular Tradition,* p. 153.
15. " 'The bloody dog is dead' replaces the customary obituary on the tragic hero; 'from the dead temples of this bloody wretch' Derby has plucked the now superfluous crown" (Wolfgang Clemen, *A Commentary on Shakespeare's "Richard III"* (London: Methuen, 1968) pp. 235–6).

NOTES TO CHAPTER 3: "THE COMEDY OF ERRORS": THE SUBLIMINAL NARRATIVE

1. Northrop Frye, *A Natural Perspective: The Development of Shakespearean Comedy and Romance* (New York: Harcourt, Brace & World, 1965) p. 77.
2. *The Riverside Shakespeare,* ed. G. Blakemore Evans (Boston, Mass.: Houghton Mifflin, 1974) p. 81.
3. Geoffrey Bullough reprints three works as sources for *The Comedy of Errors:* the *Menaechmi* of Plautus; the *Amphitruo* of Plautus; and a portion of Gower's *Confessio Amantis,* that relating to the story of Apollonius of Tyre. See *Narrative and Dramatic Sources of Shakespeare,* ed. Geoffrey Bullough, 8 vols (London: Routledge & Kegan Paul, 1957–75) I, 12–54.
4. I quote from F. A. Hirtzel's edition of Virgil (Oxford: The Clarendon Press, 1900).
5. T. W. Baldwin, citing this and the shipwreck incident, believes "that Shakspere consciously borrows from the wandering Aeneas touches for his wandering Aegeon" (*William Shakspere's Small Latine and Lesse Greeke,* 2 vols (Urbana, Ill.: University of Illinois Press, 1944) II, 487). Virgil Whitaker accepts that "The first scene is heavily indebted to Virgil's *Aeneid* for details of Aegeon's travels" (*Shakespeare's Use of Learning* (San Marino, Calif.: Huntington Library, 1953) p. 85). For a dissenting view, see J. A. K. Thomson, *Shakespeare and the Classics* (London: George Allen & Unwin, 1952) pp. 48–51: "But this line 'infandum, regina . . .' was so well known and so often quoted and imitated . . . that familiarity with it would not of itself prove acquaintance with the *Aeneid*" (p. 50). Similarly, Thomson doubts that Shakespeare read Plautus in the original.
6. A. H. Nason reproduces the record of James Shirley in the fifth form of Merchant Taylors' School. Cicero's first oration *In Catilinem* led inexorably to the second book of the *Aeneid.* See *James Shirley, Dramatist* (1915; reprt. New York: Benjamin Blom, 1967) facing p. 21.
7. John Dean, "Constant Wanderings and Longed-for Returns: Odyssean Themes in Shakespearean Romance", *Mosaic,* 12 (1978) 50–1.
8. Ibid., 50, n. 11. It is accepted that Aegeon also recalls the story Apollonius of Tyre, via Gower's version: "a moderately literate or experienced playgoer listening to Egeon's story could have responded to the echoes in it from the best known of exemplary romances, *Apollonius of Tyre*", a story which originated as a Latin romance of the third century A.D. See Leo Salingar, *Shakespeare and the Traditions of Comedy* (Cambridge University Press, 1974) p. 62 *et seq.*
9. R. A. Foakes, in his New Arden edition of *The Comedy of Errors* (London: Methuen, 1962), notes the allusion to the *Odyssey* and adds: "This line is the culmination of the images of transformation."
10. Bullough (ed.), *Narrative and Dramatic Sources of Shakespeare,* VIII, 245.

11. For the "Christianizing" idea of Ephesus, see ibid., I, 10; Foakes (ed.), *Comedy of Errors,* pp. xxix, 113–15.

12. Alex Aronson reviews the "hostile brother" motif (though without reference to *The Comedy of Errors*) in *Psyche and Symbol in Shakespeare* (Bloomington, Ind.: University of Indiana Press, 1972) pp. 113–25.

13. C. G. Jung, *Aion: Researches into the Phenomenology of Self,* 2nd edn (Princeton University Press, 1968) p. 13.

14. Frye, *A Natural Perspective,* p. 57.

15. J. C. Trewin bears down hard on such directors, in *Going to Shakespeare* (London: George Allen & Unwin, 1978) pp. 47–8: "it was not hard for a director to find appropriate emphases for a yawning Duke: 'Well, Syracusian, say *in brief* the cause' ".

16. One would naturally add the information given in the playbill, but there are always some members of the audience who do not take it in. Every box-office manager can tell strange tales of disappointed ticket-holders.

17. Baldwin, *Shakspere's Small Latine and Lesse Greeke,* I, 326.

18. The Riverside edition, like Bevington, accepts "staff" as bawdy.

19. Foakes (ed.), *Comedy of Errors,* p. 46; and E. A. M. Colman, *The Dramatic Use of Bawdy in Shakespeare* (London: Longmans, 1974) p. 187.

20. See the entries on *knock* in J. S. Farmer and W. E. Henley, *Slang and its Analogues: Past and Present* (reprt. in 3 vols, New York: Kraus Reprint, 1965); and Eric Partridge, *A Dictionary of Slang and Unconventional English,* 2 vols, 5th edn (London: Routledge & Kegan Paul, 1961).

21. It is perhaps worth noting that this play's structure depends on a "split" centre. Act III has two scenes, and not, as so often in Shakespeare, three.

22. Frye, *A Natural Perspective,* p. 58.

23. Foakes (ed.), *Comedy of Errors,* p. 16.

24. C. J. Sisson, *New Readings in Shakespeare,* 2 vols (London: Dawson, 1956) I, 93: quoted by Foakes (ed.), *Comedy of Errors,* p. 49, who also notes that a London brothel bore the name.

25. Foakes, ibid., p. 4.

26. For *zombie,* *Webster's Third New International Dictionary* has (1b) "the supernatural power or essence that according to voodoo belief may enter into and reanimate a dead body".

27. Alexander Leggatt, *Shakespeare's Comedy of Love* (London: Methuen, 1974) p. 17.

28. There are 41 references to "home" in *The Comedy of Errors,* more than for any other play in the canon.

NOTES TO CHAPTER 4: DISCOMFORT IN "THE MERCHANT OF VENICE"

1. See H. H. Furness's New Variorum edition of *The Merchant of Venice* (1888: repr. New York: Dover, 1964) p. 449.

2. Laurence Danson, *The Harmonies of "The Merchant of Venice"* (New Haven, Conn.: Yale University Press, 1977) p. 3.

3. *The Merchant of Venice,* ed. A. D. Moody (London: Edward Arnold, 1964) p. 4.

4. See John Russell Brown's note on this passage, in his New Arden edition of

The Merchant of Venice (London: Methuen, 1957).

5. Randolph Quirk, "Shakespeare and the English Language", *A New Companion to Shakespeare Studies,* ed. Kenneth Muir and Samuel Schoenbaum (Cambridge University Press, 1971) p. 70.

6. Jonathan Miller, in his production for the National Theatre (1970), left Jessica alone with Antonio at the end. A glance was exchanged between these partners in alienation, then Antonio departed, leaving the stage to Jessica. The sound of a Jewish sofar was heard.

7. I confess to being baffled by C. L. Barber's "And no other final scene is so completely without irony about the joys it celebrates" (*Shakespeare's Festive Comedy* (Princeton University Press, 1959) p. 187).

8. It is curious how so many critics still their faculties in the presence of Elizabethan Bawdy, as though it were a composite mode that invariably justified itself. The quality of bawdy depends in any society on the circumstances of its expression; and Shakespeare depicts here a finely adjusted society well capable of distinguishing between degrees of licence. Here, the coarseness of Gratiano anticipates the effect Shakespeare achieves at the end of *Troilus and Cressida,* with Pandarus's lines.

NOTES TO CHAPTER 5: "TWELFTH NIGHT": THE EXPERIENCE OF THE AUDIENCE

1. "One quart of sack and one quart of claret wine" is recorded as the refreshment with which Shakespeare entertained the visiting preacher at New Place, and for which he was reimbursed. See S. Schoenbaum, *William Shakespeare: A Compact Documentary Life* (Oxford: Clarendon Press, 1977) p. 280.

2. C. L. Barber, *Shakespeare's Festive Comedy* (Princeton University Press, 1959) pp. 249, 251.

3. See John Russell Brown, "Directions for *Twelfth Night*", in *Shakespeare's Plays in Performance* (Harmondsworth: Penguin, 1969) pp. 222–34.

4. Barber, *Shakespeare's Festive Comedy,* p. 250.

5. The alternatives need not be confined to the RSC orthodoxy of the 1970s, the presentation of Maria as an elderly spinster.

6. Barber, *Shakespeare's Festive Comedy,* p. 252.

7. These lines are touched again in Sir Toby's advice to Sir Andrew, concerning a socially explosive term: "If thou thou'st him some thrice, it shall not come amiss" (III. ii. 43–4).

8. Irving's own prompt copy, now lodged in the Folger Shakespeare Library (call-mark TN, 13) notes "crying" during the cell scene. Madeleine Bingham states that Irving "turned comedy into tragedy, especially in the last scenes, where he was deeply tragic". See her *Henry Irving and the Victorian Theatre* (London: George Allen & Unwin, 1978) p. 207.

9. Lawrence Stone's chapter on "The Peerage in Society" contains many illuminating instances of attitudes towards the gentleman (*The Crisis of the Aristocracy 1558–1641* (Oxford: The Clarendon Press, 1965) pp. 21–64). On the blurring of lines, for example, he quotes Philip Stubbes (1583): "such a confuse mingle mangle of apparell . . . that it is verie hard to know who is noble, who is worshipfull, who is a gentleman, who is not; for you shall

have those . . . go daylie in silkes, satens, damasks, taffeties and suchlike, notwithstanding that they be both base by byrthe, meane by estate & servyle by calling. This is a great confusion & a general disorder, God be merciful unto us" (p. 28). But: "Despite the blurring of the line by the devaluation of the word 'gent.', despite the relative ease with which it could be crossed, the division between the gentleman and the rest was basic to Elizabethan society" (p. 50).

10. By coupling the term with Malvolio as late as Act IV, scene ii, Shakespeare imparts to the audience that it has got an important judgement wrong on him. Nor can Malvolio's claim be dismissed: it is confirmed explicitly by Viola and Olivia (v. i. 274, 277). The insidious force of the revelation is the greater if we consider the word's history in *Twelfth Night*. There are 22 references to "gentleman", more than in any other play in the canon: the term occupies significant space in the play's consciousness. And all 16 of the references that precede Malvolio's claim are to Cesario. "Gentleman", then, is dramatically validated by its main illustration: a gentleman is what Cesario is.

11. Hugh Hunt sees him as "a second clown – a rival to the ageing Feste". See *Old Vic Prefaces* (London: Routledge & Kegan Paul, 1954) p. 77.

12. Joseph Summers, "The Masks of *Twelfth Night*", *University of Kansas City Review*, 22 (1955) 25–32.

13. Barbara K. Lewalski, "Thematic Patterns in *Twelfth Night*", in *Shakespeare Studies*, 1 (1965) 171.

14. Barber, *Shakespeare's Festive Comedy*, p. 257.

15. *The Complete Works of Shakespeare*, ed. Hardin Craig (Glenview, Ill.: Scott, Foresman, 1951) p. 642.

16. "Probably the variety of the entertainment at the Hope seemed nothing new to Londoners. All London playhouses appear to have accommodated more miscellaneous spectacle than we are accustomed to associate with theatres, and the bear-garden tradition had long been one of variety" (G.E. Bentley, *The Jacobean and Caroline Stage*, 7 vols (Oxford: The Clarendon Press, 1941–68) VI, 209). Oscar Brownstein views more sceptically the relationship between theatres, and bull- and bear-baiting yards, in "Why Didn't Burbage Lease the Beargarden? A Conjecture in Comparative Architecture", in *The First Public Playhouse: The Theatre in Shoreditch 1576–1598*, ed. Herbert Berry (Montreal: Queen's-McGill University Press, 1979) pp. 81–96.

17. They govern other variants of the bear metaphor, such as Ursula in *Bartholomew Fair*. Joel Kaplan sees her as "a roaring ursuline devil, like the comic bear-demons in *Like Will to Like* or *Mucedorus*, particularly at home in Jonson's Hope Theater used on alternate days for stage plays and bear baitings". See his "Dramatic and Moral Energy in Ben Jonson's *Bartholomew Fair*", *Renaissance Drama*, n.s.3 (1970) 144–5. Note also Macbeth's apotheosis as bear:

> They have tied me to a stake; I cannot fly,
> But bear-like I must fight the course.
>
> (v. vii. 1–2)

18. Bernard Beckerman, in his discussion of Globe staging, makes the point that "without a ranking figure . . . an object of ridicule, accusation, or pity serves as the focal point" (*Shakespeare at the Globe 1599–1609* (New York: Macmillan, 1962) p. 171). Whatever the variable geometry of the final grouping, Malvolio must be its focus during his brief appearance, after which it reverts naturally to Orsino – who, among other things, is a metamorphosis of Bear.

NOTES TO CHAPTER 6: COMMUNAL IDENTITY AND THE RITUALS OF "JULIUS CAESAR"

1. T. S. Dorsch, in his New Arden edition of *Julius Caesar* (London: Methuen, 1955) p. xlix.
2. The point does not emerge from John Ripley's coverage of the 1898 production in *"Julius Caesar" on Stage in England and America 1599–1973* (Cambridge University Press, 1980). It is, however, elaborated in the programmes of Tree's later productions of *Julius Caesar*, available in the Tree Archive at the University of Bristol Theatre Collection.
3. For a provocative review of the possibilities of that myth, see the chapter on Prometheus in Jan Kott's *The Eating of the Gods: An Interpretation of Greek Tragedy* (New York: Random House, 1974) pp. 3–42.
4. It may be worth noting that Shakespeare suppresses Plutarch's detail that Casca called upon his brother for help in the assassination. The revolt of the brothers is an unwanted dimension.
5. Nevill Coghill, *Shakespeare's Professional Skills* (Cambridge University Press, 1964) p. 62.
6. T. J. B. Spencer, "Shakespeare and the Elizabethan Romans", *Shakespeare Survey 10* (1957) 28.
7. Pierre Grimal, *The Civilization of Rome* (London: George Allen & Unwin, 1963) p. 100.
8. Cinna's joke about being a bachelor (ii. iii. 17) is not in Plutarch. I infer that this is another brush-stroke in Shakespeare's picture of an Establishment that has lost interest in having children.
9. R. H. Barrow, *The Romans* (Harmondsworth: Penguin, 1949) p. 20.
10. Dorsch (ed.), *Julius Caesar*, p. xxxv; Maynard Mack, *"Julius Caesar"*, reprinted in *Modern Shakespearean Criticism*, ed. Alvin B. Kernan (New York: Harcourt, Brace & World, 1970) pp. 292, 295.
11. John W. Velz, " 'If I were Brutus now . . .': Role-Playing in *Julius Caesar*", *Shakespeare Studies 4* (1968) 153.
12. Thomas Van Laan, *Role-Playing in Shakespeare* (University of Toronto Press, 1978) pp. 141–52.
13. Velz, " 'If I were Brutus now' ", 153.
14. Shakespeare clearly takes the Roman *cognomen* as the approximate equivalent of the English surname.
15. Ernest Schanzer, *The Problem Plays of Shakespeare* (New York: Schocken, 1965) pp. 54–5.
16. G. Wilson Knight, *The Imperial Theme* (London: Methuen, 1953) pp. 44, 61; quoted by Schanzer, *The Problem Plays*, p. 45.

17. Nicholas Brooke, *Shakespeare's Early Tragedies* (London: Methuen, 1968) p. 159.
18. Schanzer, *The Problem Plays*, p. 25.
19. Cf. the decorously Roman way in which Octavius and his followers determine the appropriate reaction to the news of Antony's death:

> *Agrippa*   Caesar is touch'd.
> *Maecenas* When such a spacious mirror's set before him,
> He needs must see himself.
> (*Antony and Cleopatra*, v. i. 33–5)

20. Richard David preserves an apt vignette from the RSC programme for *Julius Caesar* (1972), Cicero's account of a visit by Caesar. "Nerve-racking – but it passed off tolerably. He was in a very good humour. The talk at table was all of literature, and serious subjects were avoided – just a quiet man-to-man talk. Still, he wasn't the sort of guest to whom you'd say 'look me up when you're passing this way again'." See his *Shakespeare in the Theatre* (Cambridge University Press, 1978) p. 151.
21. Maurice Charney, *Shakespeare's Roman Plays: The Function of Imagery in the Drama* (Cambridge, Mass.: Harvard University Press, 1961) p. 221, note 1.
22. Dorsch (ed.), *Julius Caesar*, p. 64.
23. "Constancy", equally, is a Roman code-word. Note

> (i)   *Brutus* With untir'd spirits and formal constancy (ii. i. 227)
> (ii) *Portia* I have made strong proof of my constancy (ii. i. 299)
> (iii) *Portia* O constancy, be strong upon my side (ii. iv. 6).

24. Brents Stirling, *Unity in Shakespearian Tragedy* (New York: Columbia University Press, 1956) p. 42.
25. Shaw missed the point here. He viewed the playing of the full text as a blunder: "Brutus's reception of Messala's news, following his own revelation of it to Cassius, is turned into a satire on Roman fortitude". See G. B. Shaw, *Our Theatres in the Nineties* (London: Constable, 1932) iii, 303. Why not accept "satire" as Shakespeare's approximate intention? The "alternative version" approach brings enough difficulties. Granville-Barker justified his preference rather oddly: "By this text Brutus first hears the news from Messala, and he exhibits a correct stoicism" (*Prefaces to Shakespeare* (Princeton University Press, 1978) ii, 411). It is "correct" if Portia's death is news to Brutus, and an "incidental lie" (412) if it is not? I should have thought it equally a lie, in either case. Perhaps the real point at issue is changing attitudes towards stoicism (in its general sense). In fact, the text makes excellent sense in the theatre on its own terms. See the illuminating comments on the RSC version of 1972 in David, *Shakespeare in the Theatre*, pp. 19–20, 154.

NOTES TO CHAPTER 7: MASQUES AND DUMB SHOWS IN WEBSTER

Citations are to the Revels Plays editions by John Russell Brown of *The White Devil* (2nd edn, London: Methuen, 1966) and *The Duchess of Malfi* (London: Methuen, 1964); and to Frances A. Shirley's edition of *The Devil's Law-Case* in the Regents Renaissance Drama Series (Lincoln, Neb.: University of Nebraska Press, 1972).

1. Dieter Mehl, *The Elizabethan Dumb Show* (London: Methuen, 1965) p. 139.
2. Ibid., p. 141.
3. Frances Yates, *Shakespeare's Last Plays: A New Approach* (London: Routledge & Kegan Paul, 1975) p. 22.
4. I do not notice any close verbal parallels between the speeches in Jonson's masque and *The White Devil*, but stellar imagery is noticeably common to both. Jonson makes Arthur *discovered as a star above*. (A watercolour by Inigo Jones survives of a Masquer Lord as "A Star", 1613. It is reproduced in *Inigo Jones: The Theatre of the Stuart Court* by Stephen Orgel and Roy Strong, 2 vols (London: Sotheby Parke Bernet; Berkeley: University of California Press, 1973).) The prince/star (or comet) association occurs several times in *The White Devil*, especially in Vittoria's "This thy death / Shall make me like a blazing ominous star" (v. vi. 131–2). "Glories", a key word in Webster, occurs several times in the masque.
5. It is reproduced in Orgel and Strong, *Inigo Jones*, i, 164–5.
6. The general case is reinforced by the connections between the *Masque of Blackness* and *The Devil's Law-Case*. We can also note that Dent regards Jonson's *Masque of Queens* (1609) as furnishing a definite source for *The White Devil*, one of only two published after 1608. See R. W. Dent, *John Webster's Borrowing* (Berkeley and Los Angeles: University of California Press, 1960) p. 57.
7. The argument was first advanced by Inga-Stina Ekeblad in "The Impure Art of John Webster", *Review of English Studies*, n.s. 9 (1958) 253–67.
8. Brown (ed.), *The Duchess of Malfi*, p. xxxvi.
9. Ralph Berry, *The Art of John Webster* (Oxford: The Clarendon Press, 1972) pp. 43–5.
10. See Frank B. Fieler, "The Eight Madmen in *The Duchess of Malfi*", *Studies in English Literature 1500–1900*, 7 (1967) 343–50.
11. See G. P. V. Akrigg, *Jacobean Pageant* (New York: Atheneum, 1967) pp. 232–40.
12. *Princeton Encyclopedia of Poetry and Poetics*, ed. Alex Preminger (Princeton University Press, 1965) p. 475.
13. M. C. Bradbrook, *The Living Monument: Shakespeare and the Theatre of his Time* (Cambridge University Press, 1976) pp. 117–18.
14. James L. Calderwood, "*The Duchess of Malfi*: Styles of Ceremony", *Essays in Criticism*, 12 (1962) 137, 139.
15. Richard David, "Of an Age and for All Time: Shakespeare at Stratford", *Shakespeare Survey 25* (1972) 163.
16. Brown (ed.), *The Duchess of Malfi*, pp. xlii, 39.
17. Alexander Leggatt, private communication.
18. Akrigg, *Jacobean Pageant*, p. 150.
19. Text and numbering as given in Orgel and Strong, *Inigo Jones*, i.

20. John C. Meagher, *Method and Meaning in Jonson's Masques* (Notre Dame, Ind.: University of Notre Dame Press, 1966) p. 108.
21. Stephen Orgel, *The Jonsonian Masque* (Cambridge, Mass.: Harvard University Press, 1965) p. 120.
22. David Horowitz, *Shakespeare: An Existentialist View* (London: Tavistock, 1965) p. 130.
23. Inga-Stina Ewbank, " 'These Pretty Devices': a Study of Masques in Plays", in *A Book of Masques*, General Editors T. J. B. Spencer and S. W. Wells (Cambridge University Press, 1967) p. 434.
24. Jonas A. Barish remarks that Jonson's masques move "toward irony . . . toward a less and less convincing image of the ideal society in the ascendant". See his *Ben Jonson and the Language of Prose Comedy* (Cambridge, Mass.: Harvard University Press, 1960) p. 266. An interesting extension of this line occurs in Dale B. J. Randall's *Jonson's Gypsies Unmasked: Background and Theme of "The Gypsies Metamorphos'd"* (Durham, NC: Duke University Press, 1975). Mr Randall deals with "Jonson's use of the masque as a mode of satirical admonishment . . . Jonson's excited knowledge that this time he was playing with fire" (p. 12). This masque was highly successful (performed thrice in 1621) and Jonson seems to have got away with his metaphoric suggestion that Buckingham and "his numerous relations and friends are, figuratively speaking, a covey of gipsies" (ibid., p. 10).

NOTES TO CHAPTER 8: SHAKESPEARE AND CHIVALRY

1. The most famous reference to chivalry in the literature of England, Burke's, is a lament for its passing. The nineteenth-century revival of chivalry enacted the fate of previous waves: it collapsed during the 1914–18 War. See Mark Girouard, *The Return to Camelot: Chivalry and the English Gentleman* (New Haven, Conn.: Yale University Press, 1981).
2. Frances Yates, "Elizabethan Chivalry: The Romance of the Accession Day Tilts", *Astrea: The Imperial Theme in the Sixteenth Century* (London: Routledge & Kegan Paul, 1975) pp. 88–111.
3. Ibid., p. 108.
4. G. B. Harrison, *Shakespeare under Elizabeth* (New York: Holt, 1933) p. 219.
5. Oscar James Campbell, *Comicall Satyre and Shakespeare's "Troilus and Cressida"* (San Marino, Calif.: Huntington Library, 1938) p. 219.
6. Lytton Strachey, *Elizabeth and Essex* (New York: Harcourt, Brace, 1928) p. 35; quoted in Campbell, *Comicall Satyre*, p. 230. For a contemporary image of chivalric prowess, see Hilliard's miniature of the Earl of Cumberland, who in 1590 took over from Sir Henry Lee the office of Queen's Champion. The portrait is described by Yates, "Elizabethan Chivalry", p. 104.
7. The most celebrated recent production of *Henry V* (RSC, 1975) gave an extra dimension to the French court. Terry Hands, the director, wrote of the first French court scene:

> Up to this point, apart from the French Ambassador in scene ii, the costuming has been largely modern, the costumes drawing inspiration from both World Wars.

With the appearance of the French, a specific fifteenth century element is added. Their colours are blue, grey, gold. They are not going to war. Their entrance is stately, to harp and flute. They are obsolete. The stillness of the stageing, the follow spots, the echoing hall, suggest an etiquette-bound remnant of the age of chivalry, the age of Richard II.

Theatrically, period costume is an outmoded convention. Used here it helps to accentuate the fact that the French are frozen in an era that has already passed. (*"Henry V" for the Centenary Season at the Royal Shakespeare Theatre*, ed. Sally Beauman (Oxford: Pergamon, 1976) p. 137.

8. Campbell (*Comicall Satyre*, p. 231) identifies "a persistent critical belief that the Trojans in the play represent a fineness of feeling and nobility of endeavor which the churlish Greeks brutally destroy. But this discernment of a clear-cut moral difference between the men of the two armies is seemingly one of the misinterpretations incident to a wrong conception of the purpose of the work."

9. T. McAlindon is rather hard upon Aeneas, as guilty of periergia or "overlabour" (Puttenham). See his "Language, Style and Meaning in *Troilus and Cressida*", *PMLA*, 84 (1969) 29–43. Aeneas's address to Agamemnon (I. iii) is certainly flowery and elaborate; but there is no evidence that the challenge as worded is anything but Hector's. The insidious flattery of Aeneas's address ("If you are men of the world you will appreciate this") is successful, and the assumptions of his ceremonial style are accepted by the Greeks. The whole question of Greek-Trojan decorum is well debated by T. McAlindon and Mark Sacharoff in a later issue of *PMLA*, 87 (1972) 90–9.

10. The well-educated Elizabethan playgoer knew, of course, that Fame was destined to yield to Time and Eternity. See Alistair Fowler, *Triumphal Forms: Structural Patterns in Elizabethan Poetry* (Cambridge University Press, 1970) pp. 38, 58–9.

11. In John Barton's production (RSC, 1976), Ajax's reiterated commands persistently defeated the trumpeter's timing, so that he raised and lowered his trumpet several times before the opening blast.

NOTES TO CHAPTER 9: THE MASQUE OF "HENRY VIII"

1. G. C. D. O'Dell, *Shakespeare from Betterton to Irving*, 2 vols (New York: Scribner, 1920) II, 444–6; II, 464; Muriel St Clare Byrne, "A Stratford Production: *Henry VIII*", *Shakespeare Survey 3* (1950) 120–9.

2. J. C. Trewin, *Shakespeare on the English Stage 1900–1964* (London: Barrie & Rockcliff, 1964) p. 224.

3. Henry Fenwick, "The Production", in *The Shakespeare Plays: Henry VIII* (New York: Mayflower, 1979) p. 21.

4. John D. Cox, "*Henry VIII* and the Masque", *English Literary History*, 45 (1978) 390–409.

5. Ibid., 401.

6. "The dance of masquers and their ladies is a vital, colourful background for the meeting and Wolsey's remark that Henry is 'with dancing a little

heated', while it hints at the King's ardour, indicates that the dance has been energetic – a coranto, volta or galliard" (Alan Brissenden, *Shakespeare and the Dance* (London: Macmillan, 1981) p. 104).

7. St Clare Byrne, "A Stratford Production", 121.

8. Quoted by E. K. Chambers, in *The Elizabethan Stage,* 4 vols (Oxford: The Clarendon Press, 1923) II, 419.

9. "What Guthrie and his actors have realized . . . is that the whole passage is the grandmother and grandfather of all running commentaries" (St Clare Byrne, "A Stratford Production", 128).

10. As, apparently, happened with real masques. Chambers says that "subject to the limitations of space and the discretion of the door-keepers, the performances seem to have been open to all comers" (Chambers, *The Elizabethan Stage,* I, 205).

11. Alice S. Venezky, *Pageantry on the Shakespearean Stage* (New York: Twayne, 1951) p. 60.

Index

155